Contents

1. Geography - Page 5
2. Origins of the USA - Page 7
3. 19th Century America (Gold Rush, Wild West, Civil War and more) - Page 15
4. Inventions - Page 35
5. Landmarks & Buildings - Page 46
6. Sport - Page 55
7. Famous People - Page 64
8. Myths & Legends - Page 76
9. Holidays & Celebrations - Page 88
10. 20th Century America (World Wars, Space Exploration and more) - Page 97
11. Music & Entertainment - Page 114
12. Animals & Nature - Page 124
13. Food & Drink - Page 133
14. Culture - Page 139

WHAT ARE YOU MOST EXCITED TO DISCOVER?

INTERESTING FACTS & STORIES ABOUT THE UNITED STATES OF AMERICA

For Curious Kids!

Five Mile Publications are based in the United Kingdom, and have been passionately making a variety of books for children since 2020!

For more information, or for any enquiries, email us at hello@fivemilepublications.com

Copyright 2023 Five Mile Publications. All Rights Reserved.

Geography

The Country's Size

The USA is a massive country that lies in North America, between Mexico and Canada. Measuring at 9,833,517 sq km, is the third-largest country in the world, ahead of China, but behind Canada. Interestingly, the size of China is so close to the size of the USA, that depending on how it is measured, the USA may be listed as fourth largest country behind China.

Capital

The capital of the United States is not New York, but a place called Washington D.C. which is some 400 miles south. The D.C. stands for District of Columbia, as the city lies in its own area and not in any state. Here, you can the White House where the president lives, and monuments like Nelson's column honoring early presidents of the USA.

The Last Frontier

Alaska, nicknamed the last frontier, is a state that holds several records for the USA. The tallest mountain in the USA, and North America, is called Denali. It is 6190 meters high!
Alaska is also the largest state of the USA, but despite this, is one of the least

Geography

populated, having less than one million people living there.

Alaska, along with Hawaii, are the only two states that are disconnected from the mainland of the USA.

The fact that Alaska is so far north means that northern Alaska is the only place in the USA where in the summer, the sun never sets and at night it is completely light! Conversely, in the winter, the sun never rises and the whole day is completely dark!

Great Lakes

The Great Lakes, located on the border between the USA and Canada, are the largest group of freshwater lakes in the world. They consist of Lake Superior, Lake Michigan, Lake Huron, Lake Erie, and Lake Ontario. Some large cities lay by these lakes, including Chicago, Detroit and Toronto. Together, they are about the size of California!

Border Force

The longest border in the world is between the USA and Canada, measuring in at over 8000 miles!

Origins Of The USA

Natives

Long before Europeans came to the land now known as the United States, it was home to over 1000 different Native American tribes and nations, many of these still survive, but restricted to reservation areas created for them. These included the Apache ... and the majority of names of US states, cities and areas are based on the native name for it.

For example, the state of Oklahoma comes from the Choctaw language of the Choctaw Nation.

New Amsterdam

Long, long ago, in a bustling city we now know as New York, there was a time when it had a different name and a different story. Before it became the iconic New York City we know today, it was called New Amsterdam.

In the early 17th century, the Dutch people first arrived in what is now New York during their exploration. They came from a place called Holland in Europe, seeking new opportunities and a chance to build a prosperous colony.

They settled on the southern tip of the island we now call Manhattan, right by where the World Trade Center is, along the

Origins Of The USA

beautiful shores of the Hudson River. They built a small town and named it New Amsterdam, after their capital city in their homeland.

New Amsterdam quickly grew into a lively and vibrant place. The Dutch brought their traditions, culture, and language, as you will see in another fact throughout this book. People from all over the world came to New Amsterdam in search of a better life. The town was filled with charming houses, busy markets, and ships sailing in and out of its harbor. The Dutch were skilled traders, and they established relationships with Native American tribes and other European settlers, exchanging goods and ideas.

Life in New Amsterdam was filled with excitement and adventure. People gathered in the town square, called the Bowling Green, to celebrate, share stories, and play games. However, after tensions between European countries, in 1664, the British came and took control of the colony from the Dutch. New Amsterdam quickly became New York, named after the Duke of York, who later became King James II of England.

The British also bought their culture with them, and built impressive structures, such as Fort George and the famous St. Paul's

Origins Of The USA

Chapel.

Today, as you walk the streets of New York City, you can still find hints of its Dutch past. There are neighborhoods like Harlem and Brooklyn that have names rooted in Dutch history, as well as Dutch architecture that features thin, tall houses with triangle roofs.

Boston Tea Party

In a city called Boston, there was a special event in 1773, where the American colonies were upset with the British government. They felt that they were being treated unfairly and heavily taxed without their consent. One of the things that bothered the colonists the most was a tax on tea.

In those days, the British East India Company had a monopoly on tea, which means they had control over its trade. The British government gave them special privileges and made their tea cheaper than other tea sold in the colonies.

This made the colonists very angry because they believed it was unfair. They didn't like being told what kind of tea they could buy and at what price. They thought it was important to stand up for their rights and show the British government that they wouldn't be pushed around.

Origins Of The USA

So, on a chilly night in December, a group of colonists decided to take action. They disguised themselves as Native Americans, dressing up in blankets and feathers to hide their identities. They called themselves the Sons of Liberty.

They quietly made their way to the harbor, where British ships were carrying tea. They boarded one of the ships called the Dartmouth and started throwing chests of tea into the water. The chests floated and turned the harbor into a sea of tea!

It was a bold and daring move, and the colonists knew they were risking trouble with the British government. But they believed it was important to stand up for their rights and show that they wouldn't be controlled by unfair laws.

The Boston Tea Party sent a strong message to the British government. It showed that the colonists were united and determined to fight for their freedom and the right to govern themselves.

The British government was furious when they heard about the Boston Tea Party. They punished the people of Boston by closing the harbor and passing even stricter laws. This made the colonists even more determined to fight for their rights.

The Boston Tea Party became a symbol of

Origins Of The USA

resistance and the fight for freedom. It inspired people all across the colonies to come together and stand up against unfair laws and taxes. It was one of the important events that led to the American Revolution, where the colonies fought for their independence from Britain.

Independence Declaration

In the land that would become the United States of America, there were a group of very important men known as the Founding Fathers.

The founding fathers included:

- George Washington - The first President of the United States and helped lead the American Revolutionary War against Great Britain.
- Thomas Jefferson - The main author of the Declaration of Independence and served as the third President of the United States.
- Benjamin Franklin - A smart man who was a scientist, inventor and diplomat who helped win the war against Britain and in drafting the Declaration of Independence and the U.S. Constitution.

Origins Of The USA

- John Adams – A lawyer, diplomat, and statesman who served as the second President of the United States. He helped end the American Revolutionary War.
- James Madison: Madison is often referred to as the "Father of the Constitution" for his role in making the U.S. Constitution. He later became the fourth President of the United States.

They lived during a time when the people of the land were not happy with the way they were being treated by their rulers, the British.

These brave men believed in freedom, equality, and the right to govern themselves. They came together to discuss and plan how they could make things better for themselves and their fellow countrymen. They wanted to create a new nation, a place where everyone would be treated fairly and have a say in how they were governed.

One of the most important moments in their journey was the writing of a special document called the Declaration of Independence. It was written by a wise and thoughtful man named Thomas Jefferson. He carefully crafted the words to express the beliefs and desires of the American people.

Origins Of The USA

On a warm summer day in 1776, the Founding Fathers gathered together in a room filled with anticipation. They read the words of the Declaration aloud, and their hearts swelled with hope and determination.

The Declaration of Independence declared that the people had the right to life, liberty, and the pursuit of happiness. It stated that all men are created equal and should be treated with fairness and respect. It boldly declared that the people had the power to govern themselves and make decisions for their own future.

The signing of the Declaration was a momentous occasion. Each Founding Father took turns adding their signature to the document, pledging their lives, their fortunes, and their sacred honor to the cause of freedom.

The Declaration of Independence became the foundation for a new nation. It inspired people across the land to stand up for their rights and fight for the freedoms they believed in. It sparked a revolution that would lead to the birth of the United States of America.

The Founding Fathers' vision and courage led to the creation of a country where people could live in freedom and pursue their dreams.

Origins Of The USA

Stars And Stripes

The USA flag came to be in 1777, where the leaders of the United States gathered together to create a flag that would represent their unity and independence. Francis Hopkinson, who was a member of Congress and a skilled artist, was asked to design the first official flag. He came up with a beautiful design that had thirteen alternating red and white stripes, representing the 13 original colonies that formed the United States.

In the top left corner, Francis placed a blue rectangle, called a canton; inside of which he placed 13 stars, arranged in a circle, to symbolize the unity of the colonies.

This first flag, called the "Stars and Stripes," was a powerful symbol of freedom and independence particularly during the American Revolution.

As the years went by, more states joined the USA, and the flag needed to be updated. Each time a new state joined, a new star and a new stripe were added to the flag. Eventually, there were too many stars to fit in a circle, so they were arranged in rows, which today contain 50 stars for the 50 states that make up the USA.

19th Century America

Lewis & Clark Expedition

In the beginnings of the United States, there were two brave explorers named Meriwether Lewis and William Clark. They were chosen by President Thomas Jefferson to lead an amazing adventure called the Lewis and Clark Expedition.

The year was 1804, and the United States had just gained a large area of land called the Louisiana Purchase. President Jefferson wanted to learn more about this new land, so he asked Lewis and Clark to explore it from the Mississippi River all the way to the Pacific Ocean, a journey over 5000 miles in length and taking the men over 2 years in total! Imagine being away from civilization, only having the company of your group for 2 years!

Lewis and Clark assembled a team of skilled adventurers, known as the Corps of Discovery, and set off on their epic journey. They traveled in canoes and on foot, facing wild rivers, thick forests, and tall mountains.

Their expedition took them through unknown territories, encountering different Native American tribes, plants, and animals they had never seen before. They had to be cautious and respectful as they interacted

19th Century America

with the Native Americans, learning from them and sharing their own knowledge.

The Corps of Discovery faced many challenges along the way. They encountered rough weather, dangerous animals, and difficult terrain.

During their journey, Lewis and Clark discovered and documented many plants and animals that were unknown to the people back home. They saw majestic mountains, beautiful rivers, and wide open prairies. They mapped the land and kept detailed journals of their findings, so that others can learn from their experiences.

One of the most exciting parts of their expedition was when they reached the Rocky Mountains. They had to find their way through steep cliffs and deep valleys. But when they finally crossed the mountains, they saw a vast and breathtaking landscape, stretching as far as the eye could see.

After months of traveling and exploring, Lewis and Clark finally reached the Pacific Ocean in 1805. They had accomplished their mission, becoming the first explorers to cross the continent from the east to the west.

The journey back was filled with new adventures and discoveries. They faced new challenges, but their spirits remained high

19th Century America

as they carried with them the knowledge and treasures they had gained along the way.
In 1806, Lewis and Clark returned to the United States as heroes. Their expedition had provided valuable information about the land, the people, and the plants and animals of the western territories.
Their journey, known as the Lewis and Clark Expedition, is remembered as one of the greatest explorations in American history. It opened up new opportunities for settlement, trade, and understanding between different peoples.

The Underground Tunnel

During the early years of the USA, slavery was a common practice, where some people were treated unfairly because of the color of their skin. Amidst this period, there was a brave and determined woman named Harriet Tubman who became a symbol of hope and freedom for many people during this time.
Harriet Tubman was born into slavery herself, but she dreamed of a better world where all people could be free. She knew that she had to do something to help make that dream come true.
Harriet had a special gift—she was incredibly brave and knew how to navigate

19th Century America

through the woods without getting lost. So, she decided to use her talents to help others escape to freedom.

Harriet became the conductor of a secret network called the Underground Railroad. But it wasn't actually a real railroad with trains and tracks. It was a group of brave people who worked together to help enslaved people escape to the North, where they would be free.

At night, when the world was asleep, Harriet would guide groups of people through forests, across rivers, and past dangerous obstacles. She would tell them to follow her, like a shining North Star guiding them to safety.

Sometimes, they would walk for hours, hiding during the day to and traveling only at night. They had to be very quiet and careful so that nobody would hear or see them. It was a dangerous journey, and they had to be brave.

Harriet knew the risks involved. She faced the danger of being caught by slave catchers or other people who wanted to keep slavery alive, and she knew the punishment for escaping would likely be torture or even death for her whole group. But she never gave up, and she never stopped helping people find their freedom.

19th Century America

During her journeys, Harriet helped rescue around 70 people from slavery, including her own family. She became a hero to those she helped, a symbol of hope and courage in the face of injustice.

After the Civil War ended and slavery was abolished, Harriet continued to fight for equal rights and worked for the better treatment of others. She was a remarkable woman who showed that one person can make a difference, no matter how small or humble they may seem.

Alamo

The Battle of the Alamo is a story of bravery, sacrifice, and the fight for independence.

Long ago, Texas was actually part of Mexico, but some people in Texas wanted to be free and govern themselves. So, they decided to fight for their independence from Mexico. They gathered at a fort called the Alamo, a small mission in the town of San Antonio. Inside the Alamo were a group of brave soldiers led by legendary figures like Davy Crockett, Jim Bowie, and William B. Travis. They were determined to defend the fort and protect the independence of the people of Texas.

19th Century America

In February 1836, a Mexican army led by General Santa Anna surrounded the Alamo. The Mexican army was much larger and better equipped, but the defenders of the Alamo did not give up. They were willing to fight with all their strength and courage.

For 13 days, the defenders of the Alamo held their ground, refusing to surrender. They fought fiercely against the Mexican army, with cannons booming and gunfire filling the air. They defended the Alamo with all their might, even though they knew the odds were against them.

During the battle, brave soldiers like Davy Crockett and Jim Bowie fought with incredible courage. They inspired their fellow defenders with their bravery and determination. The defenders knew they were fighting for something bigger than themselves—their freedom and the future of Texas.

Unfortunately, on the thirteenth day, the Mexican army broke through the walls of the Alamo and they were defeated.

Although the battle resulted in the loss of the Alamo, it became a symbol of heroism and sacrifice and inspired others to join the fight for independence. Just a few weeks after the battle, the Texan army won a decisive victory over the Mexican army at

19th Century America

the Battle of San Jacinto, securing Texas independence as a new country, before quickly joining the USA as a state.

The California Gold Rush

California as we know it today was a different place when the USA was first formed. Almost nobody outside of natives lived there, and although there was beautiful nature everywhere, for most people, it was too far from where most of society was, in the east in cities like New York. But little did the people know that a remarkable discovery in 1848 was about to change everything.

One sunny day, a man named James Marshall was working at a sawmill near a river called the American River. As he was working, he noticed something shiny in the water. He bent down to pick it up and couldn't believe his eyes. It was gold! James had discovered a nugget of gold that sparkled in the sunlight.

Excited and full of wonder, James shared his discovery with everyone around him. News quickly spread like wildfire, and people from all over the world heard about the shiny gold in California. They left their homes, families, and jobs in the more developed part of the country in search of

19th Century America

the precious metal.

People traveled from far and wide, carrying their hopes and dreams in their hearts. They came by boat, wagon, and even on foot, braving long and treacherous journeys to reach California. They became known as the "Forty-Niners" because many of them arrived in the year 1849.

The gold rush brought together people from all walks of life. Miners, merchants, farmers, and even families with children all joined in the great adventure. They packed all the equipment they would need, a pan, a shovel, scales. They set up camps along the rivers and streams, hoping to find their own fortune in the golden soil.

Life in the gold fields was not easy. The days were filled with hard work, digging and panning for gold under the hot sun. Miners used special pans to wash away the dirt and rocks, leaving behind tiny particles of gold. They searched rivers, creeks, and even the mountains, hoping to strike it rich.

As more and more people arrived, new towns sprung up all over California. These towns were bustling with activity, filled with people selling supplies, building houses, and setting up businesses.

But finding gold was not guaranteed. Many miners worked tirelessly for hours, days,

19th Century America

and even months without finding much. Many people were in fact better off staying in their jobs as the gold they found wasn't even enough to pay their bills.

Yet, they persevered, driven by the hope that one day, they would strike gold. The newspaper was full of stories of people who had found gold and sold it for a fortune, and the hope that their lives could change too kept people going.

It wasn't just those digging for gold that made their fortunes. Sellers of shovels and other equipment for mining gold also made fortunes without even having to do physical work.

The gold rush in California lasted from 1848, when James Marshall first found gold to 1855, when by that point, all the easily accessible gold had been found, and the government could only find gold by mining deep into ground.

The gold rush had a significant impact on California. Towns grew into cities, and the population soared with over 300,000 new people in the space of a few years. San Francisco, once a small town of 200 people grew to a bustling city of 30,000 people between 1846 to 1852. The discovery of gold brought prosperity and opportunities for some, but it also had its challenges. The

19th Century America

land changed, and the environment suffered as people dug up the earth in search of the precious metal. Although not everyone found gold, the gold rush created a spirit of adventure and an enduring legacy. People came together from different backgrounds, cultures, and countries, creating a rich and diverse society in California. The gold rush also spurred on other gold rushes in different parts of the USA.

The Wild West

The Wild West was a period in the late 1800s when settlers moved westward in search of new opportunities and a better life. It was a time when vast open plains, towering mountains, and dusty towns captured the imagination of many. This was a place where legends were made and stories were born. Cowboys were some of the most iconic figures of the Wild West. These brave and skilled horse riders took care of cattle and guided them across the sprawling landscapes. They wore wide-brimmed hats, boots, and spurs, and rode their trusty horses through dusty trails, becoming symbols of freedom and adventure.

Wild West towns were bustling with activity. People from all walks of life flocked to

19th Century America

these towns, seeking fortune, adventure, or a fresh start. Saloons were lively places where cowboys gathered to share stories, play games, and enjoy a drink or two. Can-can dancers entertained the crowd, and musicians filled the air with lively tunes. But the Wild West wasn't just about cowboys and saloons. It was also a time of lawlessness, where outlaws roamed the land. Jesse James, Billy the Kid, and Butch Cassidy were among the notorious outlaws who captured people's imaginations with their daring heists and narrow escapes from the law.

The Wild West was also shaped by the brave women who played important roles in this rugged era. Women like Annie Oakley, known as "Little Sure Shot," were skilled markswomen who defied gender norms and showcased their talents in Wild West shows.

The stories of Native American tribes are an essential part of the Wild West too. Native Americans had lived on these lands for thousands of years and had their own rich cultures and traditions. They were skilled hunters, trackers, and horse riders, and their way of life was deeply connected to the land.

As the United States expanded westward, conflicts arose between settlers and Native

19th Century America

Americans over land and resources. These conflicts often played out in battles and skirmishes, creating tension and changing the landscape of the Wild West.

The Wild West may seem like a distant and mythical place, but its spirit lives on through stories, movies, and legends. It represents a time of exploration, courage, and the pursuit of dreams. While it had its challenges, the Wild West remains a symbol of adventure and the indomitable spirit of those who tamed the frontier.

Cowboy Culture

Wild west traditions that have lived till today include chuckwagon races, rodeos, and cowboy poetry.

Chuckwagon races look back to the days when cowboys on cattle drives relied on chuckwagons for their food and supplies. In these races, teams of horses pull old-fashioned chuckwagons around a track, showcasing their speed, agility, and teamwork. It's a thrilling and adrenaline-filled event that captures the excitement and competitiveness of the Wild West.

Rodeos are another beloved tradition that showcases various cowboy skills and events. They often feature bull riding, bronc

19th Century America

riding, barrel racing, and roping competitions. Rodeos bring together talented cowboys and cowgirls who showcase their bravery, strength, and horsemanship. These events not only entertain audiences but also honor the traditions and skills that were crucial in the Wild West era.

Cowboy poetry is a unique form of storytelling and expression. It is a heartfelt and entertaining way for cowboys and cowgirls to share their experiences, stories, and emotions through verse. These poems often touch on themes of life on the range, the beauty of nature, and the challenges faced by cowboys. Cowboy poetry gatherings are held where poets recite their work, keeping the tradition alive and giving voice to the spirit of the Wild West.

19th Century America

Civil War

The north and south of the USA were like two different worlds, each with its own way of life and beliefs. Over time, tensions grew between the two regions, and their differences threatened to tear the nation apart.

In the South, the land was vast and fertile, perfect for growing crops like cotton. To work these large plantations, the people of the South relied on enslaved Africans and their descendants. These enslaved people endured great hardships and were denied their freedom. But in the South, slavery was seen as an essential part of their economy and way of life.

In the North, things were different. The land was not as well suited for agriculture, so the people turned to factories and industries. They embraced the idea that all people should be free and equal, regardless of the color of their skin. Many people in the North fought tirelessly to abolish slavery and bring about a more just society. As time passed, the North and the South became more divided over the issue of slavery. The North saw it as injustice, while the South believed it was their right to own slaves. These disagreements

19th Century America

threatened to split the country in two. Then, in 1860, Abraham Lincoln was elected President. Lincoln believed in the idea that all people should be free, and he wanted to stop the expansion of slavery into new territories. This scared many people in the South, who believed their way of life was under attack.

One by one, Southern states decided they would no longer be part of the United States. They formed their own government, called the Confederacy, and declared their independence. The nation was on the brink of war.

In 1861, the first shots of the Civil War were fired at Fort Sumter. It was a long and brutal conflict that put brother against brother and friend against friend. Families were torn apart, and the land was stained with the blood of brave soldiers.

The war raged on for four long years. In the end, the Union, led by the North, emerged victorious. During the war, Abraham Lincoln made several popular speeches, including the Emancipation Proclamation, which made slavery illegal in the USA, as well as the Gettysburg address, that said that soldiers who died in the civil war did so to defend the freedom of the country.

19th Century America

Shopping Spree

The United States during the 19th century expanded alot, from a country along the east coast to 5x its size by the end of the century. The USA purchased alot of the land that increased it in size. Firstly, in 1803, the USA purchased French Louisiana, a massive piece of land that covers central modern USA for $15 million. Next, in 1819, the USA purchased Florida from Spain for $5 million.

As the USA progressed west, they initially offered the newly formed Mexico $25 million for the modern day region of California and other western states, but they refused and as a result, the USA went to war with Mexico, won, and claimed those territories for themselves. In 1853, the USA did offer to purchase more of Mexico for $10 million, this time Mexico did accept the offer.

The USA wasn't quite done however, and in 1867, the USA paid $7 million to Russia to acquire Alaska. Along with land that the USA has taken by force, such as Puerto Rico and Hawaii, the USA actually also made an offer to purchase Greenland from Denmark for $100 million in 1946, an offer that Denmark has rejected!

19th Century America

The Great Chicago Fire

In October 8, 1871, after weeks of hot and dry weather, a small fire started in a wooden barn owned by a woman named Catherine O'Leary. The flames grew quickly, fueled by strong winds and dry conditions. The fire spread rapidly, jumping from building to building, leaving a trail of destruction in its wake. The city of Chicago in this period was a city built from mainly wood, and so the fire effortlessly spread.

The people of Chicago were taken by surprise as the fire grew larger and more intense. Firefighters rushed to the scene, but the fire was so fierce that their efforts seemed helpless. The flames leaped across the river, devouring everything in their path.

The people of Chicago came together in a time of crisis. They formed bucket brigades, passing buckets of water from hand to hand in an attempt to put out the fire. People opened their homes to those who had lost everything, offering shelter and comfort in a time of great need.

Despite their efforts, the fire raged on for three long days where it seemed like there was no end in sight. The people of Chicago watched in sadness and disbelief as their beloved city burned.

19th Century America

Finally, rain began to fall on October 10th, the third day of the fire. It was a relief for the people, helping to extinguish the flames and bring an end to the great fire. When the smoke cleared, most of the city lay in ruins. Buildings, homes, and businesses were reduced to ashes.

But amidst the devastation, there was hope. The people of Chicago were resilient and determined to rebuild their city. Donations poured in from other US cities and from abroad. Architects, engineers, and workers from all over came to help. They designed new buildings with stronger materials to prevent future fires.

Chicago rose from the ashes, stronger and more beautiful than ever before. The city was rebuilt with wide streets, grand buildings, and modern fire safety measures. The Great Chicago Fire taught the people of Chicago and the world the importance of fire safety and preparedness. Lessons learnt from the Great Chicago fire help strengthen fire departments across the world and come up with good practices that have gone on to reduce the severity of future fires.

19th Century America

Battle of Little Bigfoot

Before the western civilization discovered America, the USA belonged to the native American people, who had a different way of life. Some such natives, known as Lakota, Cheyenne and Arapaho lived in tribes in northern USA, they mainly hunted their food to eat and lived close to nature. But there came a time when their way of life was threatened.

In the 1800s, settlers from the east began moving westward, seeking new opportunities and claiming the land as their own. The U.S. government wanted to control these vast territories, and conflicts arose between the Native Americans and the newcomers.

One summer day in 1876, tensions reached a boiling point. The U.S. Army, led by General George Armstrong Custer, set out to confront the Native American tribes and enforce the government's control. Little did they know that the tribes were ready to defend their way of life with all their might.

On the banks of the Little Bighorn River, a battle unfolded that would become legendary. Native American warriors, led by chiefs Sitting Bull and Crazy Horse, fought endlessly to protect their families, their culture, and their sacred lands.

19th Century America

As the battle raged, the Native Americans displayed bravery and determination. They were skilled horse riders and fierce warriors, using their knowledge of the land to their advantage. They fought with honor and courage, protecting their people from the advancing army.

General Custer and his men fought bravely as well, but they were outnumbered and outmatched. Despite their best efforts, they faced defeat. The Battle of Little Bighorn became known as "Custer's Last Stand," as General Custer and his soldiers were overwhelmed by the Native American warriors.

It was a bittersweet victory for the Native American tribes. They had successfully defended their way of life and their lands, but the battle came at a great cost. The U.S. Army would not forget the defeat, and it would lead to further conflicts and challenges for the tribes in the years to come, where the U.S. government would eventually enforce their rule over the land.

Inventions

I believe I can fly

In a small town called Dayton, Ohio, lived two brothers named Orville and Wilbur Wright, who had a big dream. They wanted to build a machine that could fly, just like the birds they watched soaring high in the sky.

Orville and Wilbur were curious and determined. They spent hours studying birds and how they flew. They watched their wings flap, twist, and turn, trying to understand the secret of flight.

They owned a bicycle repair shop, which they also as their workshop for their experiments, the Wright brothers started experimenting. The bicycle shop was essential for the Wright Brothers, as they believed that flying a plane would require balance from the pilot, just like cycling a bike. They built and tested many different types of gliders, small planes without engines. They wanted to learn how to control the movements of the aircraft in the air.

After years of hard work and countless experiments, the Wright brothers made an amazing discovery. They realized that the key to flying was to have a way to control the plane's movements. They invented a system called "wing warping," which allowed

Inventions

them to bend and twist the wings of their planes.

Excited by their progress, Orville and Wilbur set out to achieve their ultimate goal: powered flight. They knew they needed an engine to make their plane fly, so they designed and built their own lightweight engine.

On December 17, 1903, a historic day arrived. The Wright brothers took their newly built aircraft, called the Flyer, to a place called Kitty Hawk in North Carolina. The winds were just right, and they were ready to make history.

Orville climbed into the cockpit, and Wilbur helped him get ready for takeoff. With a deep breath, Orville started the engine, and the propellers began to spin. The Flyer started to move down a rail, gaining speed. And then, with a burst of excitement and amazement, the Flyer left the ground! It was the first powered flight in history! Orville was flying, and Wilbur watched in awe from the ground.

The flight lasted only 12 seconds, but it was a monumental achievement. The Wright brothers had shown the world that human beings could fly like birds. They had unlocked the secret of flight and opened up a whole new world of possibilities.

Inventions

Over the years, Orville and Wilbur continued to improve their designs and build better planes. They traveled around the world, demonstrating their inventions and inspiring others to pursue their dreams of flight. The Wright brothers' incredible achievement paved the way for modern aviation. Today, airplanes fill the skies, carrying people to far-off places in a matter of hours. All thanks to the determination, perseverance, and ingenuity of Orville and Wilbur Wright.

A Lightbulb Moment

Thomas Edison was a curious and imaginative person who loved to tinker with machines and explore new ideas. One day, he had a big dream - he wanted to invent a way to bring light into people's lives, even when the sun went down.
At that time, people used candles and gas lamps to light their homes, but these methods were not very safe or efficient, and he thought the new invention of electricity should make a way to make lighting easier. Thomas believed that there had to be a better way, so he set out on a mission to create a practical and reliable light source.
He spent countless hours experimenting and

Inventions

trying different materials and designs filled his workshop with all sorts of strange contraptions and gadgets. He tried using different filaments, which are like tiny wires, to see which one would work best.

After many failed attempts, and countless days, Thomas finally had a breakthrough. He discovered that a thin strip of carbonized bamboo could glow brightly when an electric current passed through it. This was the birth of the incandescent light bulb! Excited by his invention, Thomas worked tirelessly to perfect it. He made improvements to the design and experimented with different materials until he finally created a light bulb that could last for hours and provide a steady, bright light. Thomas knew that his invention had the power to change the world. He realized that it would not only light up people's homes but also transform the way people lived and worked. It would open up a whole new world of possibilities.

In 1879, after years of hard work, Thomas Edison showcased his invention to the world. He lit up a street in Menlo Park, New Jersey, with rows of his light bulbs, and people were amazed. It was a historic moment

Inventions

that would forever change the way we live. The invention of the light bulb revolutionized society. It made it possible for people to work and play late into the night! It brought safety to homes, streets, and businesses. The world became a brighter place, thanks to Thomas Edison's brilliant mind and determination.

Thomas Edison went on to invent many other amazing things, but his light bulb remained one of his most significant achievements.

Someones Calling

One day, while Alexander was working on a project to help people who were deaf hear better, he had a brilliant idea. He realized that sound could be turned into an electric signal and sent through a wire to another location. This idea sparked his imagination, and he began to work tirelessly to turn his vision into reality.

With the help of his assistant, Thomas Watson, Alexander started experimenting in a small workshop. They built many different devices and tested them one by one. They faced many challenges and had to try different materials and designs to make their invention work.

Finally, after many months of hard work and countless experiments, Alexander and Thomas

Inventions

had a breakthrough. They successfully transmitted sound from one end of a wire to the other, and they knew they were onto something big.

Excited by their discovery, Alexander rushed to the patent office to claim his invention. On March 7, 1876, he was granted a patent for the telephone. It was a historic moment because the telephone was the first device that could transmit sound over long distances, and it would forever change the way people communicated.

Soon after, Alexander demonstrated his invention at the Centennial Exhibition in Philadelphia, where people were amazed to hear voices coming from a distant location. Word of this incredible invention spread quickly, and soon, telephones started appearing in homes and offices across the country.

With the telephone, people could now speak to each other without having to be in the same room or even the same city. It connected families and friends who were far apart, and it made businesses and governments communicate more efficiently. The invention of the telephone transformed the world. It brought people closer, enabled faster communication, and made the world feel smaller.

Inventions

A Rollercoaster Ride...

In the lively city of New York, there was a place called Coney Island, known for its sandy beaches and exciting entertainment. It was in this vibrant area that the world's first-ever roller coaster was built, forever changing the world of amusement parks.

It was 1884, a time when amusement parks were just beginning to emerge as popular destinations for fun and excitement. A man named LaMarcus Adna Thompson, known as the "Father of the Roller Coaster," had a brilliant idea to create a thrilling ride that would captivate the imagination of visitors.

Thompson's creation, called the Switchback Railway, was a remarkable feat of engineering. It consisted of a series of wooden tracks, carefully designed to create a fast-paced and exhilarating experience. The ride stretched over 600 feet and reached speeds of up to 6 mph, which was considered incredibly fast at that time.

As the Switchback Railway opened its doors to the public, people flocked to Coney Island to experience the excitement firsthand. Riders climbed aboard the small, open-air cars and held on tight as the coaster climbed to its peak, sending them on

Inventions

a wild journey of twists, turns, and unexpected drops. It was a roller coaster of emotions as riders felt their hearts race with each thrilling moment.

The Switchback Railway revolutionized the concept of amusement parks. It introduced the idea of a dedicated ride purely for the purpose of adrenaline and enjoyment. People were drawn to the rush and the unique sensation of defying gravity.

The success of the Switchback Railway paved the way for amusement parks to sprout up in various locations, each featuring its own unique coaster experience.

The List Goes On

Beyond the important inventions we talked about, the USA can be proud of many more inventions that have changed the world. These include the invention of the television, by Philo Farnsworth and others, the air conditioning system, by Willis Carter, the microwave oven by Percy Spencer, the computer, invented by several inventors including Steve Jobs, the founder of Apple, and even the development of the internet. What these people had in common is that they asked questions about the world around them, and what can be done to improve it.

Inventions

Unusual Inventions from the USA

Besides the major inventions, here are some lesser known ones:

- The Pogo Stick - a fun invention that lets you bounce up and down like a kangaroo! It was invented by George Hansburg in 1919. You can hop around and have a great time with this bouncy invention.
- Silly Putty - a stretchy, squishy, and fun material that was invented by accident! In the 1940s, a scientist named James Wright was trying to create a synthetic rubber. Instead, he made this strange substance that could bounce, stretch, and even copy pictures from newspapers.
- Slinky - a toy that seems to magically walk down stairs or glide from hand to hand. It was invented by Richard James in the 1940s. The Slinky is a coiled spring that loves to move and wiggle, providing lots of fun and entertainment.
- Super Soaker - a water gun that can shoot water really far! It was invented by Lonnie Johnson in the 1980s. With a Super Soaker in your hands, you can have exciting water fights and stay cool on hot summer days.

Inventions

- Pet Rock - a very unusual invention. It was created by Gary Dahl in the 1970s. It's simply a rock that comes with a small box and instructions on how to take care of your new "pet." People thought it was funny and bought them as a silly joke!
- The Chia Pet - a little planter that grows sprouts that look like hair! Invented by Joe Pedott in the 1980s, you can water the Chia Pet and watch the sprouts grow, creating funny and unique hairstyles for your little plant friend.
- Bubble wrap - a sheet of plastic with air bubbles trapped inside. Invented by Marc Chavannes and Alfred Fielding in the 1950s, it was initially intended as textured wallpaper, but people discovered it was more fun to pop the bubbles (and that it was more useful for packaging)!

Early Automobiles

Up until the early 20th century, transportation relied mainly on horses and horse-drawn carriages. But inventors and engineers dreamt of creating a self-propelled vehicle that could revolutionize travel, one of who was Henry Ford.
Henry Ford was born in 1863 on a farm in

Inventions

Michigan, USA. By 1896, Henry Ford built his first car, called the Quadricycle. It was a simple vehicle powered by a gasoline engine and featured bicycle-like tires. Although it was a modest start, it ignited Ford's passion for automobile manufacturing. In 1903, Henry Ford established the Ford Motor Company, which aimed to produce affordable, mass-produced automobiles for the average person. His vision was to make cars accessible to everyone and transform transportation as we know it.

One of Ford's most significant contributions to the automobile industry came with the introduction of the Model T in 1908. It was the first automobile produced on an assembly line, which allowed for faster and more efficient production. The Model T was affordable, reliable, and easy to drive, making it a huge success. Ford's innovative manufacturing methods made it possible to produce cars at a lower cost, making them more accessible to a wider range of people. With the success of the Model T, Ford popularized the concept of the automobile, and car ownership became a reality for many families. Ford's production methods not only made cars affordable but also revolutionized manufacturing processes across various industries.

Landmarks & Buildings

The Statue Of Liberty

A long time ago in France, there was a young sculptor named Frédéric Auguste Bartholdi. Frédéric loved to create beautiful works of art that would make people smile and feel inspired. One day, he received a special invitation from the Americans.

The Americans wanted Frédéric to help them create a gift for their country, a gift that would symbolize freedom and friendship between nations. They wanted a grand statue that would stand tall and proud, overlooking the sparkling waters of New York Harbor. Frédéric was thrilled and honored to be a part of such an important project.

Frédéric started working tirelessly, sketching and sculpting different ideas. Finally, he came up with the perfect design. He wanted to create a statue of a strong woman, holding a torch high in her hand. The torch would represent the light of freedom, guiding all who seek a better life.

But Frédéric needed help to bring his vision to life. He asked his good friend Gustave Eiffel, who was a brilliant engineer, for help. Together, they worked day and night, planning and creating every detail of the statue as they wanted it to be magnificent and meaningful.

Landmarks & Buildings

Frédéric traveled to the small island called Bedloe's Island, where the statue would be placed. He imagined how it would look, standing there with its proud face and flowing robes, greeting ships arriving from all around the world.

To raise money for the construction of the statue, Frédéric and Gustave held fundraisers in both France and the United States. People from all walks of life, including children, donated their hard-earned pennies to support this grand project. It became a symbol of hope and unity for people from both countries.

Finally, after years of hard work and determination, the statue was ready. Frédéric and Gustave packed the statue in crates and sent it across the ocean to its new home in America. It was a long and exciting journey.

When the crates arrived in New York Harbor, everyone eagerly gathered to witness the unveiling of this magnificent gift. As the covers were lifted in 1886, the statue was revealed in all its glory.

The statue was named "Liberty Enlightening the World," but it quickly became known as the Statue of Liberty. People from all over he world came to see it, amazed at it's

Landmarks & Buildings

presence and the message it represented: freedom, equality, and the dream of a better life.

Gustave Eiffel, after the construction of the Statue of Liberty, would go on to help build the Eiffel Tower in Paris in 1887. Since that day, the Statue of Liberty has stood as a beacon of hope, welcoming millions of immigrants to the United States. It has become a symbol of America, reminding everyone that no matter where they come from, they can find freedom and a chance to pursue their dreams.

The Empire State Building

In the bustling city of New York, there was a dream to build a skyscraper that would touch the sky. This dream came true in the form of the magnificent Empire State Building, an iconic structure that stands tall and proud even today.

It all began during the 1920s, a time when people were fascinated by the idea of reaching new heights. Architects William F. Lamb and Shreve, Lamb & Harmon worked together to design the Empire State Building, a structure that would be the tallest in the world.

The construction of the building started in 1930, and it was no small task. The workers

Landmarks & Buildings

had to dig deep into the ground to lay a solid foundation, just like building a strong castle. The foundation was made of concrete and steel, ensuring that the building would stand strong against the forces of nature.

The workers faced many challenges as they built the Empire State Building. They had to brave harsh weather conditions, work at dizzying heights, and lift heavy materials, all without the safety of todays technology. The classic photo of workers sitting on a steel beam having lunch with a view over New York says it all!

But they were determined to bring the dream to life.

To reach the sky, they built a steel frame for the building. It was like assembling a giant puzzle, carefully connecting steel beams to create the framework that would support the weight of the structure. The workers used cranes and ropes to lift the heavy materials high into the air, piece by piece.

The Empire State Building also needed windows to let in the sunlight and give people a view of the city below. The workers carefully installed hundreds of windows, making sure they were strong and secure.

Landmarks & Buildings

As the building grew taller and taller, the dream was slowly becoming reality. Finally, after just over a year, the Empire State Building was complete. It stood proudly at an enormous height of 1,454 feet (443 meters) and became the tallest building in the world! It became a symbol of progress and a testament to the ingenuity of those who built it.

The Empire State Building quickly became an iconic landmark, drawing visitors from all over the world. It has been featured in movies such as King Kong, admired in photographs, and cherished by the people of New York as a symbol of their city's spirit. Even today, the Empire State Building stands as a testament to the power of dreams and the determination to reach new heights. It reminds us that with hard work, perseverance, and a little bit of imagination, we can achieve incredible things.

However, it is no longer the tallest building in New York, since 2012, the tallest building became the One World Trade Center, which stands where the twin towers previously stood at a crazy 1,776 feet (541 m)!

Landmarks & Buildings

The Fastest Rollercoaster

From humble beginnings in Coney Island - fast forward to today at Six Flags Great Adventure in Jackson, New Jersey, stands a colossal structure that reaches for the sky. It is the world's tallest roller coaster, Kingda Ka!

Rising above the park's landscape, Kingda Ka stands at a towering height of 139 meters (456 feet), equivalent to a 45-story building.

The journey aboard Kingda Ka begins with a sense of anticipation and excitement. Riders buckle into their seats, holding onto the secure restraints, eagerly awaiting the experience that lies ahead. As the countdown begins, the train accelerates from 0 to an astonishing speed of 128 mph in a jaw-dropping 3.5 seconds, an acceleration faster than any supercar you can buy. Contrast this with the first rollercoaster ever built!

The intense speed and height of Kingda Ka create an adrenaline rush like no other. It offers a heart-pounding experience that tests the bravery of riders, providing a rush of exhilaration that lingers long after the ride comes to an end.

Landmarks & Buildings

Disneyland

Once upon a time, in the magical world of imagination, there was a man named Walt Disney. He had a dream to create a place where children and adults could step into a world of enchantment and wonder. This is the story of how Disneyland came to be.

In the early 1950s, Walt Disney had already enchanted the world with his beloved characters and animated films. But he wanted to bring those stories to life in a whole new way, through a magical theme park where people could walk into the worlds he had created.

Walt's dream was met with skepticism by many. People thought it was impossible to create such a place, but Walt was determined to make his dream a reality. He searched for the perfect location and found a parcel of orange groves in Anaheim, California. It was there that the magic would begin.

With a team of talented artists, engineers, and dreamers, Walt set out to design and build Disneyland. Construction began in 1954, and just one year later, on July 17, 1955, the gates to Disneyland swung open for the very first time.

The opening day of Disneyland was a grand event. Families and children gathered to

Landmarks & Buildings

experience the wonders that awaited them. They explored different lands, like Main Street, Adventureland, Fantasyland, and Tomorrowland. They went on thrilling rides, met their favorite Disney characters, and enjoy the parades and live shows.
Disneyland quickly became a place of joy, where dreams came true. It inspired people to believe in magic and taught them that with imagination and determination, anything is possible. Walt's vision of creating a place where families could make lifelong memories had come to life.
As the years went by, Disneyland grew and evolved. New lands and attractions were added, such as Pirates of the Caribbean, Haunted Mansion, and Space Mountain. It became a place where people from all over the world could come together to celebrate the magic of Disney.
Today, Disneyland continues to inspire visitors of all ages. It has inspired the creation of other Disney theme parks around the world, spreading the magic far and wide. The story of Disneyland is a reminder that dreams can come true. It teaches us to embrace our imagination, to believe in the power of storytelling, and to never stop dreaming.

Landmarks & Buildings

Did you know?

Besides the buildings and structures already mentioned, here are some other ones that made records:

- One World Trade Center: Standing at a symbolic height of 1,776 feet (541 meters), this building in New York City is the tallest building in the Western Hemisphere!
- Gateway Arch: Located in St. Louis, Missouri, this is the tallest arch and the tallest man-made monument in the Western Hemisphere, standing at 630 feet (192 meters)!
- Hoover Dam: Located on the border between Nevada and Arizona, it is one of the tallest dams in the world, standing at 726 feet (221 meters).
- Golden Gate Bridge: The iconic Golden Gate Bridge in San Francisco, California, held the record as the longest suspension bridge span in the world when it was completed in 1937. It spans 1.7 miles (2.7 kilometers).
- Willis Tower: Formerly known as the Sears Tower, the Willis Tower in Chicago, Illinois, held the title of the tallest building in the world for 25 years. It stands at 1,451 feet (442 meters) and has 108 floors.

Sport

American Football

Long ago, in the late 19th century, a game called football was gaining popularity in the United States. However, it looked quite different from the game we know today as American football.

At that time, a game called rugby was being played in England. Rugby involved players carrying and passing a ball by throwing it, and it was a rough and physical sport. Some American colleges started playing their own version of rugby, but it had its own set of rules.

In 1869, the first-ever college football game was played between Rutgers and Princeton. This game had different rules from rugby, but it was still quite different from the American football we know today.

As the years went by, people started to think of ways to make the game more exciting and safer. They wanted to create a uniquely American version of the sport. In 1876, the Intercollegiate Football Association was formed to establish standardized rules for college football.

One important figure in the development of American football was Walter Camp. He was a coach and writer who had a significant impact on shaping the game. Walter Camp

Sport

helped create rules such as the line of scrimmage, downs, and the concept of the quarterback.

Over time, American football continued to evolve and gain popularity. People started forming professional teams, and in 1920, the National Football League (NFL) was established as the premier professional football league in the United States.

American football captured the hearts of people all across the country. It became a beloved sport that brought communities together, filled stadiums with cheering fans, and inspired athletes to showcase their skills and teamwork.

The game of American football is played with two teams trying to score points by carrying or throwing the ball into the opposing team's end zone. It requires strength, speed, strategy, and teamwork.

Today, American football is a big part of American culture. It is played at the college and professional levels, with the Super Bowl being the most-watched sporting event in the country. The sport has also spread globally, with fans and players from around the world joining in the excitement.

Sport

The Origins Of Baseball

The story of baseball begins in the early 1800s, when people in America played a game called "rounders." Rounders was a simple game where players hit a ball and ran around bases to score points. It was a popular game, especially among children.

As time went on, people started to add their own twists and rules to rounders. They began using a smaller ball and changing the way the game was played. It was during this time that baseball started to take shape.

Alexander Cartwright was one of the pioneers that designed baseball into the game we know today. He was a baseball enthusiast who wanted to create a set of formal rules for the game. In 1845, Cartwright and his friends came together to write the "Knickerbocker Rules," which became the basis for modern baseball. These rules included using a diamond shaped field with bases 90 feet apart, nine players on each team and that the ball must be pitched, not thrown.

With the rules in place, baseball began to spread throughout the country. It was played in neighborhoods, schools, and even on professional teams. People fell in love with the excitement of hitting the ball, running the bases, and making incredible catches. Baseball became known as "America's Pastime," a game that brought people together and created a sense of community. Families and friends would gather at ballparks, cheering for their favorite teams and players.

Basketball

In the late 19th century, a man named Dr. James Naismith was searching for a new sport to keep his students active during the long, cold winters. He wanted to create a game that could be played indoors and would help the students develop their physical skills and teamwork.

One day, Dr. Naismith had a brilliant idea. He decided to hang up two peach baskets on opposite ends of the gymnasium, and he wrote down a set of thirteen basic rules for the new game. And with that, basketball was born.

The first game of basketball was played on December 21, 1891. It was a simple game, with nine players on each team and a soccer ball used as the first basketball. The objective was to throw the ball into the opposing team's peach basket to score points.

Sport

As the game gained popularity, people started to realize the need for improvements. The bottom of the peach baskets was removed, and a net was added to catch the ball after each successful shot. The soccer ball was replaced by a leather ball with laces to improve its grip. Basketball began to spread to schools and colleges across the United States. In 1936, basketball made its debut as an Olympic sport at the Berlin Games, and it has been an Olympic event ever since.

Over time, the game evolved, and new techniques and strategies were developed. Players began to showcase their skills through dribbling, passing, and shooting. Teams competed fiercely, and basketball became a sport that captured the imagination of fans everywhere.

In the 1940s and 1950s, professional basketball leagues were formed, and the game continued to grow in popularity. The National Basketball Association (NBA) was established in 1946 and has become one of the most prestigious basketball leagues in the world.

Today, basketball is played in almost every corner of the globe. It has given rise to legendary players like Michael Jordan,

Sport

LeBron James, and Kobe Bryant, who have inspired millions with their incredible skills and passion for the game. Basketball has become more than just a sport. It is a symbol of teamwork, determination, and the power of dreams. Whether played on neighborhood courts or in packed arenas, basketball brings people together, fostering friendships and a sense of community.

American Racing

In 1947, a man named Bill France had a vision to organize and unify stock car racing. Stock cars are ones that are not modified much for racing, particularly if you compare it to other types of racing like Formula One. He believed that this thrilling sport could be taken to new heights with proper rules, regulations, and a governing body. And so, NASCAR, which stands for National Association for Stock Car Auto Racing, was born.

The first official NASCAR race took place in 1949 in Charlotte, North Carolina. Drivers from all around the country came together to compete, showcasing their skills and bravery. The race was a huge success, and it marked the beginning of a new era in motorsports.

Sport

As the years went by, NASCAR grew in popularity. More drivers joined the sport, and fans flocked to racetracks to witness the exhilarating races. NASCAR introduced new rules, safety measures, and innovative technologies to make the sport even more exciting and competitive.

In the 1970s and 1980s, NASCAR races started to be televised, allowing fans to watch the thrilling action from the comfort of their homes. The sport gained a loyal following, and its popularity continued to soar.

Today, NASCAR is one of the most popular motorsports in the world. It features high-speed races on oval tracks, where drivers showcase their skills, strategy, and nerves of steel. Famous drivers like Dale Earnhardt, Richard Petty, and Jeff Gordon have become legends in the sport, inspiring future generations of racers.

NASCAR has also embraced technology and innovation. Cars have become faster, safer, and more efficient. The sport has expanded beyond the United States, with races held in different countries, attracting fans from all corners of the globe.

But at its core, NASCAR remains a celebration of speed, skill, and the love of racing. It brings people together, creating a sense of community among fans and drivers alike. The roar of the engines, the smell of burning rubber, and the sight of cars zooming by at incredible speeds create an electrifying atmosphere that cannot be matched.

US Record Breakers At The Olympics

- Michael Phelps: Michael Phelps is the most decorated Olympian of all time, winning a total of 28 Olympic medals, including 23 gold medals. He broke numerous records in swimming events, including the most gold medals won in a single Olympics (8) and the most career Olympic medals.
- Simone Biles: Simone Biles is a phenomenal gymnast who has set records in artistic gymnastics. She holds the record for the most gold medals won by a female gymnast in a single Olympics (4) and the most world championship medals won by a female gymnast (25).
- Carl Lewis: Carl Lewis is an American track and field athlete who won a total of 9 Olympic gold medals. He held the record for the most consecutive gold medals won in the long jump (4) and also won gold in sprinting events.

Sport

- Jackie Joyner-Kersee: Jackie Joyner-Kersee is one of the greatest female athletes in history. She won six Olympic medals, including three gold medals in heptathlon and long jump. Joyner-Kersee's long jump record from the 1988 Olympics stood for over 30 years.
- Katie Ledecky: Katie Ledecky is a dominant force in swimming, particularly in freestyle events. She has set multiple world records and won a total of 7 Olympic gold medals, making her one of the most successful swimmers in history.
- Jesse Owens: Jesse Owens made history at the 1936 Berlin Olympics, winning four gold medals in track and field events.
- Mark Spitz: Mark Spitz is a former swimmer who won 7 gold medals at the 1972 Munich Olympics, setting a record for the most gold medals won in a single Olympics. His achievement stood for 36 years until it was surpassed by Michael Phelps.

Famous People

The Worlds Tallest Man

Robert Wadlow was a remarkable person who holds the title of the world's tallest person in recorded history. He was born in Alton, Illinois, in 1918. As Robert turned just a few months old, it was clear that he was growing at an extraordinary pace.

By the time he turned just 7 years old, he already stood at a towering height of 5 feet 10 inches (178 cm), which is the height of an average male. His rapid growth was attributed to a condition called hyperplasia of his pituitary gland, which caused excessive production of growth hormones.

Throughout his life, Robert faced many challenges due to his towering height. Simple tasks like finding clothes and shoes that fit him properly became a struggle. He often required custom-made garments and special shoes to accommodate his extraordinary stature. He even had a desk at school custom made for him.

Despite the difficulties he faced, Robert had a gentle and kind-hearted nature. He embraced his uniqueness and used his height as an opportunity to inspire others and raise awareness for the challenges faced by individuals with physical differences.

During his lifetime, Robert Wadlow became a

Famous People

well-known figure and embarked on numerous public appearances, drawing crowds wherever he went. People were fascinated by his incredible height and wanted to catch a glimpse of the world's tallest person. Robert's record-breaking height was recorded when he was 22 years old, where he was measured at a whopping 8 feet 11.1 inches (272cm)!

Tragically, soon after this measurement, Robert's life was cut short due to an infection caused by a blister. He wore braces to support his weight, but unfortunately, one was placed incorrectly and cut into his ankle.

Robert Wadlow's legacy lives on as a symbol of resilience and embracing one's uniqueness. His story reminds us that our differences should be celebrated rather than shunned.

Famous People

Becoming The President

The United States has no king or queen or prime minister. Instead, the president is the leader of the United States and is elected by the people. Being the President is a big responsibility, just like being the captain of a sports team or the leader of a club, but for over 300 million people!
The President lives and works in an iconic place called the White House.
One of the main jobs of the President is to make sure the country is running smoothly. They listen to the concerns and needs of the people and try to make the country a better place by working on important issues like education, healthcare, and the environment. The President also encourages people to be kind, respectful, and to help each other.

To become the President, a person needs to be at least 35 years old and a natural-born citizen of the United States. For their service, the president gets paid a massive $400,000 as a salary!
Every four years, people across the country vote in an election to choose who they want to be the next President. It's a big event, and people get to have a say in who leads the country.

Famous People

Being the President is not always easy. The President has to make tough decisions and face challenges, but they have a big heart and a strong desire to make the United States a better place for everyone. They inspire us to dream big, work hard, and be good citizens.

Abraham's Penny

Abraham Lincoln, before he became president of the United States, lived in a town called Springfield. Abraham was known for his tall stature and his kind heart. He had a special quality about him — he was always honest. Abraham worked at a store, where he helped customers find what they needed. One day, a customer came in and bought some items. As Abraham was counting the money, he accidentally put an extra penny in his pocket. He didn't realize his mistake until later.

Abraham could have easily kept the penny for himself, thinking that no one would notice. But that wasn't how Abraham lived his life. He believed in doing the right thing, no matter how small.

So, even though it was getting late and the store was about to close, Abraham decided to go after the customer. He wanted to return

Famous People

the penny that he had accidentally taken. He walked a long way, searching for the customer's house.

Finally, Abraham found the customer's house and knocked on the door. When the customer opened the door, he was surprised to see Abraham standing there, holding out a penny. Abraham explained what had happened and how he had come all this way just to return it. The customer was amazed by Abraham's honesty and integrity. He thanked Abraham and told him that he appreciated his honesty more than anything else. He said that Abraham had shown him the true meaning of honesty and integrity.

Word of Abraham's honesty quickly spread throughout the town. People admired him for his integrity and began to see him as a trustworthy person. They respected him for his commitment to doing the right thing, no matter how small or insignificant it seemed. Abraham's story of the honest penny became well-known, and it taught people the importance of honesty and integrity in their own lives. It showed them that even the smallest acts of honesty can have a big impact on others.

Abraham Lincoln went on to become one of the greatest presidents of the United States. He led the country through a difficult time and

Famous People

worked tirelessly to bring equality and freedom to all people.

Amelia Earhart

Once upon a time, in a world filled with dreams and adventure, there was a remarkable woman named Amelia Earhart. She was a true pioneer who showed the world that anyone, regardless of their gender, could soar to great heights. Let's embark on a journey and discover the inspiring story of Amelia Earhart!

Amelia Earhart was born on July 24, 1897, in Atchison, Kansas. As a young girl, she had a curious mind and a fearless spirit. She loved to explore and imagine all the incredible things she could do in life.

Amelia's love for flying began when she was just a little girl. She saw an airplane for the first time and was mesmerized by its grace and power. From that moment on, she knew she wanted to be a pilot and soar through the sky like a bird.

As she grew older, Amelia faced many challenges and obstacles. In a time when society believed that flying was only for men, Amelia didn't let that stop her. She worked hard, saved money, and took flying lessons. In 1921, she earned her pilot's

Famous People

license, becoming one of the first women to do so.

Amelia didn't just stop at being a pilot; she set out to break records and push boundaries. In 1932, she achieved an incredible feat by becoming the first woman to fly solo across the Atlantic Ocean. Her courage and determination inspired people around the world.

Amelia's thirst for adventure was unquenchable. She set her sights on even more daring challenges. In 1935, she became the first person, male or female, to fly solo from Hawaii to California across the Pacific Ocean.

Amelia Earhart became a household name, capturing the hearts of people everywhere. She used her fame to encourage other women to pursue their dreams and to prove that they could accomplish anything they set their minds to.

Tragically, in 1937, during an attempt to fly around the world, Amelia's plane disappeared over the Pacific Ocean. Her disappearance remains a mystery to this day, and she became a symbol of courage and determination.

She proved that with determination, passion, and a belief in oneself, one can achieve greatness.

Famous People

I'm Not Giving Up My Seat

rosa Park's story is one of courage and standing up for what is right.

In those days, there were unfair rules that said African Americans had to sit in the back of the bus and give up their seats if a white person wanted to sit. Rosa Parks knew that this was not fair and wanted to make a change.

One day, after a long day of work, Rosa boarded a bus and found a seat in the designated "colored" section. As the bus filled up, the driver told Rosa and others to give up their seats for white passengers. But Rosa, tired of the injustice, made a brave decision. She decided to stay seated and refuse to give up her seat, knowing that she could be arrested for her act of defiance. Ultimately, after being removed by police officers, the news of her actions sparked a big movement. Rosa's actions led to a boycott of the city buses by African Americans, led by a young minister named Martin Luther King Jr. People walked or carpooled instead of taking the bus, showing their determination to fight for equal rights.

Rosa's courage caught the attention of the whole country, and sparked the Civil Rights

Famous People

Movement that would eventually see equal rights for all.

Oprah Winfrey

From a young age, Oprah had a passion for learning and storytelling. She loved reading books and performing in school plays. But life wasn't always easy for her. Oprah faced many challenges and obstacles along the way. When Oprah was just a child, her family didn't have much money. They didn't have a television, so Oprah would use her imagination to create her own stories and shows. She dreamed of one day having her own TV show, where she could inspire and help others.

Oprah's journey wasn't always smooth. She faced hardships and even endured difficult times in her childhood. But she never gave up on her dreams. She believed in herself and knew that she had a voice that needed to be heard.

In her teenage years, Oprah moved to Nashville, Tennessee, to live with her father. There, she got her first job in radio and discovered her natural talent for connecting with people through the power of words.

After finishing high school, Oprah pursued a career in broadcasting. She started working

Famous People

as a news anchor and reporter, and her charisma and ability to relate to people quickly made her a rising star in the industry.

In 1986, Oprah launched her own talk show called "The Oprah Winfrey Show." It became a huge success, making Oprah a household name. Her show touched the lives of millions of people, tackling important issues, inspiring viewers, and giving a platform to voices that needed to be heard.

But Oprah didn't stop there. She used her success and influence to make a difference in the world. She started her own production company, Harpo Productions, and became a philanthropist, supporting causes like education and women's empowerment.

Oprah's impact extends far beyond the television screen. She has been recognized as one of the most influential women in the world, and her generosity and kindness have touched countless lives.

The story of Oprah Winfrey teaches us the power of believing in ourselves, following our passions, and never giving up. It shows us that with hard work, determination, and a compassionate heart, we can overcome any obstacle and achieve our dreams.

Famous People

Elvis Presley

Elvis Presley, the King of Rock and Roll. From a young age, Elvis loved music. He would listen to the sounds of gospel, country, and rhythm and blues, and he dreamed of becoming a singer. Elvis was always a bit different from the other kids, with his unique style and the way he moved when he danced.

When Elvis was just a teenager, he and his family moved to Memphis, Tennessee. It was there that his music career would take off. One day, he walked into a recording studio called Sun Records and sang a few songs for the owner, Sam Phillips. Sam was amazed by Elvis' voice and his passion for music. He knew that Elvis had something special.

In 1954, Elvis recorded his first song, "That's All Right." The song had a unique sound that blended different styles of music. People couldn't help but move and groove to his music. They had never heard anything like it before.

Elvis became a sensation, capturing the hearts of teenagers and adults alike. His energetic performances and signature dance moves, like his famous hip-shaking, drove his fans wild. He had a voice that could make you smile, laugh, or cry, all in one song.

Famous People

Elvis released hit after hit, songs like "Heartbreak Hotel," "Jailhouse Rock," and "Hound Dog." His music changed the world of music forever. He brought rock and roll to the forefront, mixing different genres and creating a sound that was uniquely his own. But Elvis wasn't just a great singer; he was also a kind and generous person. He loved his fans and always tried to make them happy. He starred in movies, performed in sold-out concerts, and became a global superstar.

Sadly, in 1977, Elvis passed away, but his music and legacy continue to live on. He has influenced countless musicians and artists who followed in his footsteps. His songs are still loved and cherished by people all around the world.

Myths & Legends

The Legend Of Bigfoot

Once upon a time, deep in the wilderness of the United States, there was a legendary creature known as Bigfoot. Bigfoot was said to be a tall and hairy creature, resembling a giant ape, that roamed the forests, leaving behind mysterious footprints and capturing the imagination of many.

The legend of Bigfoot has been passed down through generations, with stories and sightings dating back for hundreds of years. Many people believe that Bigfoot is real and still lives hidden in the vast wilderness of North America.

One of the most famous stories about Bigfoot takes us to the Pacific Northwest, a region known for its beautiful forests and towering mountains. It is said that Bigfoot makes its home there, deep in the dense forests where few humans venture.

In the early 1900s, reports of strange encounters with a large, hairy creature started to emerge. People claimed to have seen footprints much larger than any human could make. Some even claimed to have seen Bigfoot with their own eyes, describing a creature covered in long, dark hair and standing as tall as a tree.

As the legend of Bigfoot grew, scientists

Myths & Legends

and adventurers became intrigued. They set out to investigate these sightings and find evidence of the elusive creature. They examined footprints, studied eyewitness accounts, and even set up cameras to capture a glimpse of Bigfoot.

Despite their efforts, Bigfoot remained a mystery, always one step ahead, leaving behind only footprints and blurry photographs. Some people believe that Bigfoot is a gentle giant, a creature of the forest who wants to remain hidden and live in harmony with nature. Others think Bigfoot is a guardian, protecting the wilderness and its creatures from harm.

The legend of Bigfoot continues to capture the imagination of many, inspiring stories, movies, and even dedicated researchers who spend their lives searching for clues. Some say that finding Bigfoot would unlock the secrets of the natural world and deepen our understanding of the wonders that still exist in the wild.

Do you think Bigfoot is real or simply a creature of myth and folklore?

Myths & Legends

Area 51

Situated deep in the Nevada desert, there was a mysterious place called Area 51. It was a secret and heavily guarded military base that sparked the curiosity of people around the world.

Area 51 was surrounded by tall fences and warning signs, keeping prying eyes away. Many wondered what secrets lay hidden within its borders.

Some people believed that Area 51 was a place where the government studied and kept evidence of UFOs. They imagined alien spaceships and extraterrestrial beings hidden away behind closed doors.

One event supporting this idea is the Roswell UFO sighting. Four years prior to the building of Area 51, in 1947, a mysterious object crashed on a ranch owned by a man named Mac Brazel. The crash caused a great deal of excitement and confusion in the area. Rumors spread quickly, and some believed that an alien spacecraft had crashed to Earth.

The local military base, Roswell Army Air Field, became involved in the investigation. Initially, the military released a statement claiming they had recovered a "flying disc." which fueled speculation and excitement

Myths & Legends

about the possibility of alien life. However, just a day later, the military suddenly changed their statement, saying it was a weather balloon that had crashed instead, which to this day is still their official stance.

This sudden change in the official explanation caused even more intrigue and led to a variety of theories, none of which are confirmed, but could suggest that Area 51 is currently housing the "flying disc". Other people thought that Area 51 was a top-secret laboratory, conducting experiments and developing advanced technology far beyond what the world knew. They imagined brilliant scientists working on incredible inventions and discoveries.

Although the details of what truly goes on in Area 51 remain classified and undisclosed, what we do know is that it has been a place where the United States government tests and develops advanced aircraft and technology.

Area 51 has fueled people's imaginations and led to many stories and speculations. It reminds us that there are still mysteries in the world, waiting to be discovered. It sparks our curiosity and encourages us to explore, question, and seek answers.

Myths & Legends

The Disappearing Man

There are mysteries that are still unsolved to this day in the United States, one of which is the story of a mysterious man named D.B. Cooper. His story, known as the Mystery of D.B. Cooper, began on a fateful day in 1971.

D.B. Cooper wasn't his real name. It was a pseudonym that he used when he hijacked an airplane. You see, D.B. Cooper boarded a plane in Portland, Oregon, just like any other passenger, but he had a secret plan in mind.

During the flight, D.B. Cooper handed a note to the flight attendant, demanding a ransom of $200,000 and four parachutes. He told the crew that if his demands weren't met, he would blow up the plane.

The brave crew did their best to stay calm and follow D.B. Cooper's instructions. They landed the plane in Seattle, where the ransom was delivered. D.B. Cooper released the passengers and some of the crew, but he kept a few crew members on board.

Once the plane was in the air again, D.B. Cooper did something very daring. He put on one of the parachutes, opened the back door of the plane, and jumped out into the night sky, disappearing into the darkness.

Myths & Legends

Nobody knows for sure what happened to D.B. Cooper after he jumped. Despite an extensive search, he was never found, and the mystery of his fate remains unsolved to this day. The only clue that was found was some of the $200,000 laying by a river close to the site where D.B. Cooper jumped. No parachute, no items or footprints were ever found.
People have speculated and come up with many theories about what might have happened. Some believe that D.B. Cooper died during the jump, while others think he managed to escape and start a new life somewhere far away. What do you think?

The Story Of Coyote

Coyote was not an ordinary animal - he possessed great intelligence and was often seen as a trickster. He played a significant role in Native American folklore, where he appeared in many stories and legends. According to Native American tales, Coyote was a shape-shifter, capable of transforming himself into different animals or even humans. He had a playful nature and loved to test the boundaries of the world. Sometimes, Coyote used his powers to help others, while other times, he caused chaos and mischief. In the legends, Coyote taught important

Myths & Legends

lessons through his adventures. He taught about the consequences of greed, the importance of being humble, and the value of using wit and cunning to overcome challenges. Coyote was known for his cleverness, often outsmarting other animals or even humans.

One popular story tells of how Coyote stole fire from the powerful beings in the sky and brought it down to Earth, providing warmth and light for the people. In another tale, Coyote played pranks on other animals but learned valuable lessons about respect and humility.

Coyote was a fascinating character because he embodied both good and mischievous qualities. His stories were not only entertaining but also carried important teachings about the balance of nature and the consequences of our actions.

Alcatraz

On an island in the middle of San Francisco Bay, there is a famous prison called Alcatraz. It was known as "The Rock" because it was situated on a rocky island that made it very difficult to escape.

Alcatraz was not an ordinary prison. It housed some of the most dangerous criminals

Myths & Legends

in the USA. People who broke the law and committed serious crimes were sent to Alcatraz to keep them away from society and to keep others safe.

The prison was built in the early 1900s and operated until 1963. It had very high walls, guard towers, and strong iron bars on the windows. The prisoners were locked in small cells and were closely watched by guards to make sure they didn't try to escape.

Escaping from Alcatraz was considered nearly impossible. The prison was surrounded by freezing water, strong currents, and the distance to the mainland was quite far. However, there were a few brave prisoners who attempted to escape. One famous escape attempt happened in 1962, when three prisoners disappeared from their cells and were never found. It remains a mystery whether they made it to freedom or not.

Life on Alcatraz was tough for both the prisoners and the guards. The prisoners had strict schedules, and they had to follow rules and behave themselves. They had limited contact with the outside world and were not allowed to see their families very often. But they did have a small library and a small yard where they could exercise and get some fresh air.

Myths & Legends

Today, Alcatraz is a popular tourist attraction. Visitors can take a boat ride to the island and explore the prison. They can see the cells where the prisoners lived, the dining hall where they ate, and even the exercise yard where they spent their free time. It's an opportunity to learn about the history of the prison and imagine what life was like for those who were incarcerated there.

There was an attempt

In June 1962, three prisoners named Frank Morris, John Anglin, and Clarence Anglin made a daring attempt to escape from Alcatraz. They carefully planned their escape for months, using their intelligence and resourcefulness to outsmart the prison's security measures.

The first step of their plan involved digging holes in the walls of their cells using simple tools like spoons and a homemade drill made from a vacuum cleaner motor. They concealed their progress by creating fake vents to hide the holes. It took them many nights of work and patience to complete the holes.

Once they were out of their cells, the escapees climbed through a ventilation shaft that led to the roof. From there, they used

Myths & Legends

a homemade raft made of raincoats to brave the treacherous waters of the San Francisco Bay. They had carefully crafted life vests from rubber raincoats and even made a paddle using scrap wood.

To confuse the authorities, they left behind realistic-looking dummy heads made from plaster, human hair, and soap wax in their beds to make it appear as if they were still sleeping. This gave them a head start before the prison guards discovered their absence during the morning headcount.

The escape took place in the darkness of the night, using the cover of fog to conceal their movements. The prisoners had timed their escape to coincide with a low tide, hoping it would minimize the strength of the currents. However, the water was still freezing, making it incredibly challenging to swim to the mainland.

The escape attempt triggered an intense manhunt, with law enforcement agencies searching tirelessly for the fugitives. Despite extensive efforts, no trace of the escapees was ever found. Some speculate that they might have drowned in the cold waters, while others believe they may have successfully reached land and evaded capture.

To this day, the fate of Frank Morris, John

Myths & Legends

Anglin, and Clarence Anglin remains a mystery. Their escape attempt has got people worldwide guessing, leading to books, documentaries, and even movies about their escape.

The Legend Of Pecos Bill

Once upon a time, in the wild and untamed American West, there lived a legendary figure known as Pecos Bill. Pecos Bill was no ordinary cowboy. He was larger than life, with incredible strength, unmatched courage, and a spirit as big as the open prairies. According to the tall tales and legends, Pecos Bill was said to have been born in Texas, but he was no ordinary baby. He was born in a wild thunderstorm, and when he let out his first cry, it was so loud that it created the famous Pecos River. From that moment on, it was clear that Pecos Bill was destined for greatness.

As he grew older, Pecos Bill showed his remarkable skills and abilities. He could ride any horse, no matter how wild or unruly. Legend has it that he even rode a tornado, using it like a wild stallion, and tamed it with his incredible cowboy skills. He could rope a mountain lion, wrestle a grizzly bear, and outshoot any sharpshooter in the West.

Myths & Legends

Pecos Bill's adventures were as vast as the American frontier. He dug the Rio Grande River with his bare hands to provide water for thirsty settlers. He discovered the secret of the cactus, making it a valuable source of water in the desert. And he even lassoed the moon, pulling it closer to Earth so that people could enjoy its beauty each night.

But perhaps Pecos Bill's most famous companion was his loyal horse named Widow-maker. Widow-maker was no ordinary horse either. It was said that he could run faster than the wind and jump over mountains with a single leap. Together, Pecos Bill and Widow-maker would roam the open plains, taking on any challenge that came their way.

Pecos Bill's legendary feats and larger-than-life personality made him a beloved figure in American folklore. His stories were passed down from generation to generation, filling the hearts and imaginations of children and adults alike with wonder and adventure.

Holiday & Celebration

The Origin Of Thanksgiving

The origin of thanksgiving dates back a long, long time ago, in a land called Plymouth Colony. There were some brave people who came from England, called the Pilgrims, and they traveled across the vast ocean in a big ship called the Mayflower. The Pilgrims were seeking a new home where they could freely practice their own religious beliefs. After a long and difficult journey, they arrived in a place they called Plymouth, in what is now Massachusetts.

Life in Plymouth was not easy. The Pilgrims faced many challenges, including harsh winters, unfamiliar surroundings, and shortages of food. But they were determined and worked together to build their new community.

One year after their arrival, in the autumn of 1621, something special happened. The Pilgrims had successfully harvested their crops for the first time, allowing them to be able to sustain themselves, and they wanted to celebrate and give thanks for their blessings. They invited their Native American friends, the Wampanoag tribe, to join them in a feast of gratitude.

The Wampanoag people had been living in the

Holiday & Celebration

area for generations and taught the Pilgrims important skills like farming and fishing. They helped the Pilgrims survive and thrive in this new land. So, the Pilgrims wanted to show their appreciation by sharing a bountiful meal together.

The feast was a joyous occasion, filled with laughter, friendship, and gratitude. The Pilgrims and the Wampanoag people sat together, enjoying a feast that included wild turkey, fish, corn, pumpkins, and other delicious foods.

This special gathering became known as the First Thanksgiving. It was a time when people from different backgrounds came together to celebrate the harvest and express their gratitude for the blessings in their lives.

The First Thanksgiving was just the beginning. Over time, the tradition of Thanksgiving spread and became an important holiday in the United States. It is a day when families and friends come together to share a special meal, express their gratitude, and appreciate the blessings in their lives.

Holiday & Celebration

Was Santa Claus born in the USA?

Long ago, in a faraway land, there lived a kind and generous man named Saint Nicholas. He was known for his love of children and his passion for giving gifts. Saint Nicholas lived during the 4th century in a place called Myra, which is now part of modern-day Turkey.

Legend has it that Saint Nicholas became famous for his acts of kindness. He would secretly leave gifts for those in need, especially children. People loved and respected him so much that his legacy continued long after he passed away.

As time went on, stories of Saint Nicholas spread across different countries and cultures. Each place had its own unique way of celebrating him and his generous spirit. In some places, people would leave their shoes out on the eve of his feast day, hoping to find small gifts in them the next morning.

In the 17th century, Dutch settlers in America brought their traditions and stories of Saint Nicholas with them. They called him "Sinterklaas," and their celebrations involved gift-giving and joyful festivities. Over time, Sinterklaas evolved and transformed into the beloved figure we now

Holiday & Celebration

know as Santa Claus. The modern image of Santa Claus was shaped by the creativity and imagination of many people.

One of the most influential figures in shaping the modern Santa Claus was a man named Clement Clarke Moore. In 1822, he wrote a famous poem called "A Visit from St. Nicholas," which is also known as "The Night Before Christmas." This poem described Santa Claus as a jolly, plump man who traveled in a magical sleigh pulled by reindeer and delivered gifts to children on Christmas Eve.

In the mid-1800s, an artist named Thomas Nast started drawing illustrations of Santa Claus for newspapers. He gave Santa his iconic red suit, white beard, and round belly. These illustrations helped solidify the popular image of Santa Claus that we know today.

As time went on, Santa Claus became a central figure in Christmas celebrations around the world. Children would write letters to him, leave out cookies and milk on Christmas Eve, and eagerly await his arrival with gifts.

Holiday & Celebration

Happy Halloween!

Halloween is a fun and spooky holiday that is celebrated on October 31st. It has a fascinating history that goes back thousands of years.

The origins of Halloween can be traced back to an ancient Celtic festival called Samhain (pronounced sah-win). The Celts were people who lived in what is now Ireland, Scotland, and other parts of Europe.

Samhain was a time when the Celts celebrated the end of the harvest season and the beginning of winter. They believed that on the night of October 31st, the boundary between the living and the spirit world became blurred.

During Samhain, the Celts would light bonfires and wear costumes made from animal hides. They believed that these costumes would protect them from wandering spirits and otherworldly creatures.

As time went on, the traditions of Samhain merged with Christian beliefs. In the 9th century, the Catholic Church designated November 1st as All Saints' Day, a day to honor saints and martyrs. The evening before, October 31st, became known as All Hallows' Eve, which eventually evolved into Halloween.

Holiday & Celebration

When Irish and Scottish immigrants came to the United States, they brought their Halloween traditions with them. Over time, Halloween in America became a mix of different cultural influences, blending Celtic customs, European traditions, and local practices.

Today, Halloween is a festive holiday where children and adults dress up in costumes. Trick-or-treating is a popular tradition where children go from house to house, saying "Trick or treat!" and collecting candy. It's an opportunity to show off creative costumes and have fun with friends and neighbors.

You might also see jack-o'-lanterns, which are carved pumpkins with candles inside. This tradition comes from an old Irish folktale about a man named Stingy Jack who tricked the devil and was forced to wander with a carved-out turnip as his only source of light.

Halloween is a time for spooky decorations, haunted houses, and stories of witches, ghosts, and monsters. People also enjoy watching scary movies and reading spooky books during this time of year.

So, as you celebrate Halloween and go trick-or-treating, remember the ancient traditions that have shaped this fun holiday. It's a

Holiday & Celebration

time to let your imagination run wild, dress up in creative costumes, and enjoy the thrill of the season. Happy Halloween!

Fat Tuesday

Mardi Gras is a very exciting and colorful festival that takes place in many cities around the world, but it is most famously celebrated in New Orleans, Louisiana, in the United States. The origins of Mardi Gras can be traced back to very old traditions and celebrations.

Mardi Gras means "Fat Tuesday" in French and is the day before Lent begins. Lent is a time when people traditionally give up something they enjoy or make a special effort to be kind and thoughtful.

Hundreds of years ago in medieval Europe, people would celebrate Mardi Gras as a way to have fun and enjoy themselves before the more serious time of Lent started. They would eat rich and delicious foods, wear costumes, and have big parades. It was a time for people to come together and celebrate before the more somber period of Lent began.

When French explorers came to the area that is now Louisiana in the United States, they brought their traditions and customs with

Holiday & Celebration

them, including Mardi Gras. Over time, the celebration became a part of the culture in Louisiana, particularly in New Orleans. Today, Mardi Gras in New Orleans is known for its vibrant parades, music, dancing, and colorful costumes. People wear masks and throw beads and other fun things to the crowds. There are big floats decorated with beautiful designs and lots of delicious food to enjoy.

The Fifth Of May

The story of Cinco de Mayo begins in the year 1862, during a time when Mexico was facing a big challenge. A powerful army from France had invaded Mexico, led by Emperor Napoleon III. The Mexican people, led by General Ignacio Zaragoza, bravely fought against the French in a battle called the Battle of Puebla.

On May 5th, 1862, something extraordinary happened. The Mexican army, although small in number, managed to defeat the much larger and better-equipped French army. It was a moment of great victory and celebration for the people of Mexico. This battle became known as the Battle of Puebla, and it marked an important turning point in Mexican history.

After the battle, Cinco de Mayo became a

Holiday & Celebration

symbol of Mexican pride and resilience. It reminded the people of Mexico that they were capable of standing up against great challenges and fighting for their freedom. Over time, as more Mexican immigrants came to the United States, they brought the tradition of celebrating Cinco de Mayo with them.

Today, Cinco de Mayo is surprisingly mainly celebrated in the USA, where over the past few decades, it has spread beyond. aholiday for Hispanic people. In Mexico, despite being the ones who won that war, celebrate the day much less than in the USA.

The time is a celebration of parades, music, dancing, and delicious Mexican food. People come together to remember the bravery of the Mexican people and to celebrate the unity and strength of the Mexican community.

20th Century America

Why did the USA fight in WW1?

At the beginning of WW1, the USA decided to remain neutral and not get involved in the war. However, as the war went on, the USA started to feel the effects of the conflict. German submarines were attacking American ships that were trying to deliver goods to other countries, and many Americans were upset about this. In 1915, Germany would sink the passanger ship RMS Lusitania, killing 1198 people, many of who were from the USA.

The final straw came in 1917 when the Germans sent a telegram to Mexico trying to convince them to attack the USA! This telegram, known as the Zimmermann Telegram, was intercepted by the British and shared with the Americans. The USA was angry by this and declared war on Germany in April 1917, helping the UK and France win against Germany and the Central Powers in 1918.

20th Century America

The Prohibition Era

Once upon a time, in the early 20th century, a remarkable event called Prohibition took place in the United States. This was a time when the production, sale, and consumption of alcoholic beverages were prohibited or made illegal.

The story of Prohibition begins with a belief held by many people that alcohol was causing many problems in society. They thought that by getting rid of alcohol, they could make their communities safer and happier. So, in 1920, the government passed a law called the 18th Amendment, which made the manufacturing, sale, and transportation of alcoholic beverages illegal across the entire country.

However, something unexpected happened. Instead of stopping people from drinking, Prohibition led to a rise in illegal activities. People called "bootleggers" began making their own alcohol in secret places called "speakeasies." They would hide these speakeasies in basements or behind secret doors, and people would go there to enjoy a drink.

One of the most famous bootleggers of the time was Al Capone. He became a powerful and wealthy figure by illegally selling alcohol

20th Century America

and running underground bars. He is commonly shown as a gangster or mobster in the media, and a feared person in Chicago. The police and government tried to stop him, but he proved to be very difficult to catch.

As time went on, people began to see that Prohibition was causing more harm than good. Crime rates were rising, and the government was losing a lot of money because they couldn't collect taxes from alcohol sales. So, after about 13 years, the government realized that Prohibition was not working, and they decided to end it.

In 1933, the 21st Amendment was passed, which repealed the 18th Amendment and ended Prohibition. This allowed people to legally drink alcohol again, and the country celebrated this newfound freedom.

20th Century America

The Great Depression

Once upon a time, in the 1930s, there was a difficult period in the United States called the Great Depression. It was a time when many people faced challenges and hardships, and this is the story of the Great Depression, as told for a 10-year-old child. In the years leading up to the Great Depression, everything seemed wonderful. People were filled with hope and happiness, and life was bustling with excitement. But then, something unexpected happened that changed everything.

The stock market, where people bought and sold ownership in companies, experienced a sudden crash. This meant that many people lost their money, and businesses began to struggle to survive. People lined up in front of banks to withdraw their savings, only to find that they couldn't because of how the bank operates, they don't physically have their customers money as they lend it out. Can you imagine that?

People lost their jobs, and families had a hard time finding enough food and basic things they needed to live.

During this time, parents did their best to take care of their children, even though they were worried about how to provide for

20th Century America

them. Some families had to leave their homes and move to places where they could find work and support their loved ones.

Despite the difficulties, people came together to help one another. Communities set up soup kitchens where those in need could get a warm meal. People shared what little they had with their neighbors and supported each other during these tough times.

Even children like you played an important role during the Great Depression. They helped their families by working small jobs, such as delivering newspapers or helping with household chores. They learned to be resourceful and appreciate the simple things in life.

During this time, the government also stepped in to help. They created programs and initiatives to provide jobs and support to those who were struggling. They worked hard to bring the country out of the economic crisis and give people hope for a brighter future. One of the things that actually helped the country recover was making alcohol legal again. During the great depression, alcohol was made illegal to sell in what was known as Prohibition, but after being made legal, businesses made more money, the government collected more tax and

20th Century America

the country healed itself faster!

Pearl Harbor

It was a sunny morning on December 7, 1941, when a surprise attack took place that would forever be remembered as the Pearl Harbor Attack.

Pearl Harbor was a naval base located in Hawaii, where many American ships and planes were stationed. The people there were going about their daily lives, unaware of the danger that was about to come their way.

Early that morning, without any warning, Japanese airplanes swooped down from the sky and began to bomb the ships and the base. It was a sudden and devastating attack.

The people of Pearl Harbor, including brave sailors, soldiers, and civilians, found themselves in the midst of chaos and destruction. Explosions rocked the harbor, ships were sinking, and planes were engulfed in flames.

The attack lasted for hours, and when it finally ended, the damage was extensive. Many lives were lost, and numerous ships were damaged or destroyed. It was a dark and heartbreaking day for the United States.

The Pearl Harbor Attack was a turning point in history as it caused the United States to enter World War II, as they joined forces

20th Century America

with their allies to fight against the forces of injustice and protect freedom. Arguably, without the participation of the United States, the war may not have been won.

The Japanese motivation for attacking Pearl Harbor was to prevent the USA from interfering with their conquest. Japan was conquering most of Asia in 1941, just like Germany was conquering most of Europe, and did not want the USA to prevent them. Unfortunately for Japan, their actions only made things worse for them.

I'll be gone for a while mom!

During World War II, many young boys wanted to fight for their country and be seen as heroes. One of those boys was Calvin Graham. He was just 12 years old when he decided to lie about his age and join the U.S. Navy in 1942.

At first, Calvin was assigned to a ship as a mess attendant, but he eventually transferred to the USS South Dakota, a battleship that was part of the Pacific Fleet. During his time on the ship, Calvin saw a lot of action. He manned a machine gun during several battles, including the Battle of Guadalcanal, where the South Dakota was hit by enemy fire.

20th Century America

Despite being in the middle of a war, Calvin managed to keep up with his studies and even completed eighth grade while onboard the ship. However, his time in the Navy was short-lived. In 1943, Calvin's true age was discovered, and he was discharged from the Navy. He was just 13 years old at the time.

Duped

During World War 2, the U.S. government had a clever idea to trick the Germans into thinking that they were going to invade France from a different location. They created a fake army and made it seem like it was a real army, with fake tanks, airplanes, and even fake soldiers! This operation was called "Operation Fortitude."

The idea behind the operation was to fool the Germans into thinking that the real invasion of France was going to happen in a different location than where it actually was. This would confuse the Germans and give the real invading army a better chance of success. To make the fake army seem real, the U.S. government used a variety of tricks and strategies.

For example, they built fake tanks out of wood and canvas, and placed them in strategic locations where the Germans would be able to see them. They also had airplanes fly over the area, dropping fake paratroopers to make it seem like the invasion was really happening. Meanwhile, the real invasion was happening in a completely different location, catching the Germans off guard.

Nuclear Tests

During the 1950s and 1960s, scientists and the government in the United States were interested in learning more about nuclear energy. They believed it could be used for various purposes, such as generating electricity and creating powerful weapons. To understand nuclear energy better, the United States conducted a series of nuclear tests. These tests involved setting off atomic bombs in specific areas, often in remote places like deserts, where fewer people lived.

The purpose of these tests was to study the effects of nuclear explosions and to learn more about the power of atomic energy. For these tests, the USA would sometimes build houses and even neighborhoods, filled with all the things you might find in your own house, a fridge, a television, sofa, closets and all but without people. The house would

20th Century America

be full of mannequins, and nuclear tests would blow up these buildings to see the impact of atomic bombs on different things. During these tests, scientists gathered important data about nuclear reactions, energy release, and the impact of the explosions on the environment. Whilst the scientists learned more about how to make cleaner energy than coal and gas, the nuclear tests also had consequences. The explosions created a lot of heat, light, and radiation, which could be harmful to living things. Some people who were near the test sites experienced health problems later in life due to exposure to radiation.

The explosion clouds could be seen as far away as Las Vegas, a big city in the desert. As time went on, people became more aware of the dangers associated with nuclear testing and the potential harm it could cause to the environment and human health and of course, this led to changes in the way nuclear tests were conducted.

20th Century America

I Have A Dream

On August 28, 1963, Dr. Martin Luther King Jr. delivered his historic "I Have a Dream" speech at the Lincoln Memorial in Washington, D.C. during the March on Washington for Jobs and Freedom. This speech is considered one of the most iconic speeches in American history and a defining moment of the Civil Rights Movement. The March on Washington was a massive political rally that brought together over 200,000 people from all over the country to advocate for civil rights and economic equality for African Americans. Dr. King was one of several civil rights leaders who spoke at the event, but his speech became the most memorable and impactful. In his speech, Dr. King expressed his vision for a future where all people are judged by the content of their character, not the color of their skin. He spoke of the need for unity, and called for an end to discrimination and segregation. Dr. King's powerful delivery captured the spirit of the Civil Rights Movement and inspired millions of people to join the struggle for justice and equality.

20th Century America

Space Race

In the 1960s, a competition known as the Space Race emerged between the United States and the Soviet Union, the predecessor to Russia we know today.

It was a race to conquer the unknown depths of outer space, and both countries were determined to be the first to achieve extraordinary accomplishments and establish themselves as technologically superior.

The Space Race began with the Soviet Union taking an early lead. In 1957, they successfully launched the first artificial satellite, Sputnik 1, into orbit around the Earth. This kind of satellite would be able to be used for transmitting radio and communications worldwide. This remarkable achievement sent shockwaves throughout the United States and ignited a sense of urgency to catch up and surpass their rivals in space exploration.

In response, the United States established the National Aeronautics and Space Administration (NASA) in 1958, dedicating resources and brilliant minds to propel their space program forward. A young and charismatic American president, John F. Kennedy, set an audacious goal: to put a man on the moon before the end of the 1960s.

20th Century America

The USA embarked on a series of space missions that pushed the boundaries of human exploration. Astronauts were launched into space aboard the Mercury and Gemini spacecraft, taking significant steps toward understanding the challenges of living and working beyond the Earth's atmosphere.

You may already know the Apollo 11 was the first rocket to land on the moon, but did you know that there were many rocket launches to the moon before that?

In 1967, there was a planned launch of Apollo 1, which was called AS-204 at the time. The three astronauts onboard the rocket were doing training when a fire broke out in the cabin and sadly killed the astronauts. The mission was aborted, and in their honor, the NASA space program renamed their mission to Apollo 1.

Despite this setback, the USA was determined to beat the Soviet Union in getting a man on the moon, and so within just over a year, NASA launched unmanned rockets Apollo 4, 5, 6 and then manned rocket Apollo 7 to enter space. Apollo 8 became the first flight to leave Earth's orbit and reach the moon, although it never landed. Apollo 9 and apollo 10 also left Earth's orbit and prepared NASA for their big moment.

20th Century America

The Moon Landing

By 1969, something incredible happened. It was a moment that would go down in history and inspire people around the world. It was the year when human beings set foot on the moon!

The story begins with three brave astronauts: Neil Armstrong, Buzz Aldrin, and Michael Collins. They were part of a special mission called Apollo 11, with a mission to land on the moon.

On July 16th, a giant rocket called Saturn V launched from Earth, carrying the astronauts and their spacecraft, named the Eagle. They embarked on a journey of over 240,000 miles, leaving their home planet behind.

As the spacecraft traveled through space, the astronauts looked out the window and saw the beauty of Earth from a distance. It was a breathtaking sight, with the blue oceans, white clouds, and green land.

After several days, the Eagle approached the moon. Neil Armstrong and Buzz Aldrin climbed into a small lunar module, leaving Michael Collins in orbit around the moon in the command module.

On July 20th, the moment of truth arrived. The lunar module slowly descended to the moon's surface, and everyone held their

20th Century America

breath. The world watched and waited anxiously as Neil Armstrong carefully piloted the spacecraft towards a smooth landing.

The Eagle touched down gently on the moon's surface. Neil Armstrong radioed back to Earth the famous words, "That's one small step for man, one giant leap for mankind." With those words, Neil Armstrong became the first person to set foot on the moon. He and Buzz Aldrin explored the moon's surface, collecting rocks, taking pictures, and planting the American flag to mark their historic achievement.

People all around the world watched in awe and wonder. It was a moment of celebration and triumph. The moon landing showed us that human beings are capable of reaching for the stars, of exploring places beyond our own planet.

On July 24th, the astronauts safely splashed down in the ocean, greeted by cheers and applause. They had successfully completed their mission, returning home as heroes.

20th Century America

Why did the Vietnam War happen?

The Vietnam War started in the 1950s and lasted until 1975. It took place in Vietnam, a country in Southeast Asia. To understand its origins, we need to go back in time to when Vietnam was under French rule.

For many years, Vietnam was controlled by France, but the Vietnamese people wanted to be independent and govern their own country. This desire for independence led to a conflict between the Vietnamese and the French, known as the First Indochina War. After many years of fighting, the Vietnamese forces, led by a man named Ho Chi Minh, defeated the French in 1954. As a result, Vietnam was divided into two parts: North Vietnam, which was led by Ho Chi Minh and supported by communist countries, and South Vietnam, which was supported by the United States and other non-communist countries. This division was at a time when the Cold War was ongoing, where the world was split into two political ideologies, communism and capitalism. The USA was capitalist, and and did not want countries falling to communism, and therefore began sending military advisors and supplies to South Vietnam to help fight against the communist forces in the North. Over time, the conflict

20th Century America

escalated, and more American soldiers were sent to fight in Vietnam. The war became a long and costly struggle.

The Vietnam War was unique because it was fought in unfamiliar terrain, and the guerilla tactics used by the North Vietnamese forces made it difficult for the United States to win.

The war also led to protests and divisions within the United States, as many people questioned the involvement and the impact of the war.

Ultimately, the Vietnam War ended in 1975, nearly 20 years after it had started, when the North Vietnamese forces captured the capital city of South Vietnam, Saigon. This marked the reunification of Vietnam under communism.

Today, the country of Vietnam is still technically communist, but alot more open and friendly than during the Cold War.

Music & Entertainment

Hollywood

Long ago, in the late 19th century, Hollywood, located in California was just a small community with orange groves and open fields. The weather was warm and pleasant, making it a perfect location for outdoor activities and, as people would soon discover, for making movies. In those days, the movie industry was centered in New York City. Filmmakers would travel there to make their movies, but they faced many challenges. The weather was unpredictable, and the bustling city made it difficult to shoot scenes in peace. One day, a group of filmmakers had an idea. They thought about the sunny skies, beautiful landscapes, and friendly communities they had seen in Hollywood, and they realized it would be a perfect place to make movies. So, they packed their cameras, lights, and costumes and headed west to Hollywood. As more filmmakers arrived in Hollywood, they built studios and started making movies. The natural beauty of the area, with its palm trees, mountains, and nearby beaches, provided a stunning backdrop for the stories they wanted to tell. One of the earliest and most famous movie

Music & Entertainment

studios in Hollywood was called Universal Studios. It opened its doors in 1912 and became known for making thrilling movies that captivated audiences around the world. As more studios were built, Hollywood started to grow. Actors, actresses, directors, and other talented people flocked to Hollywood, hoping to make their mark in the movie industry. They brought their creativity, talent, and dreams, transforming Hollywood into the glamorous and exciting place we know today.

Over the years, Hollywood became the heart of the movie industry, producing countless films that entertained and inspired people worldwide. It gave birth to many iconic actors and actresses, like Charlie Chaplin, Marilyn Monroe, and Tom Hanks, who became famous stars.

Today, Hollywood is not just a place; it is a symbol of the magic of movies. The famous Hollywood Sign, which sits on a hill overlooking the city, is an iconic symbol recognized around the world.

Music & Entertainment

Smashing Records

Since the birth of Hollywood, the music and entertainment industry have gone on to smash records over and over. Here's some of Americas most impressive accomplishments:

- Best-selling album of all time: Michael Jackson's "Thriller" holds the record with over 66 million copies sold.
- Highest earning concert tour: U2's "360° Tour" holds the record for earning over $736 million.
- Highest earning media franchise, earning a massive $76.4 million comes from the Japanese owned Pokemon. The highest US media franchise is Mickey Mouse & Friends, earning $52.2 billion, just ahead of Star Wars!
- Best selling video game of all time, selling 230 million copies as of 2022, actually comes from the Swedish-created Minecraft, a creative open world game where you mine and craft. The US based Grand Theft Auto V comes in at second, selling over 180 million copies worldwide! The game is open world, based on cities that resemble popular US cities such as New York and Los Angeles, and you can drive around in a range of different cars and perform different tasks.

Music & Entertainment

- Most Academy Awards won by a movie: "Titanic" and "The Lord of the Rings: The Return of the King" share the record for the most Academy Awards won by a film, with 11 Oscars each.
- Longest-running animated TV series: The Simpsons is the longest running show in history, with over 700 episodes. The Simpsons, a cartoon that follows a "typical" American family, first aired on TV in 1989 and new episodes are still being made today, showing how much people love the show.
- Most-viewed music video on YouTube: Luis Fonsi and Daddy Yankee's "Despacito" holds the record, with over 8 billion views as of 2022! The song, sang in Spanish and translates to "Slowly", was recorded in Miami by Puerto Rican singer Luis Fonsi. When released, the song did well, and attracted Justin Bieber to do a remix, where he sang in Spanish for the first time, boosting its popularity further.
- Highest earning movie of all time: Avatar currently holds the record, earning over $2.8 billion worldwide as of 2022! The movie was released in 2009, and made use of cutting edge visual effects and was one of the first movies to be 3D.

Music & Entertainment

Birthplace of Hip Hop

Hip hop music originated in the 1970s in the United States, particularly in the neighborhoods of Bronx, New York City. It was born out of the creativity and expression of African American and Latino communities who wanted to share their stories, experiences, and struggles through music and dance.

At that time, the Bronx was facing economic challenges, and young people found joy and inspiration in the power of music. DJs, or disc jockeys, played a significant role in the development of hip hop. They would use turntables to mix and scratch records, creating unique sounds and beats.

One of the pioneers of hip hop was DJ Kool Herc. He hosted parties where he would play and mix different music genres, and people would dance to the beats. DJ Kool Herc's parties became known for their energetic and lively atmosphere, where people would breakdance and show off their skills.

Another important figure in the birth of hip hop was Grandmaster Flash. He introduced new techniques in DJing, such as using headphones to cue up the next record and using the crossfader to create smooth transitions between songs. These innovations

Music & Entertainment

helped shape the sound and style of hip hop music.

As hip hop grew in popularity, other elements became part of the culture. MCs, also called rappers would use their voices and lyrics to tell stories, express emotions, and engage with the crowd.

Graffiti artists would create vibrant and colorful artworks on walls, expressing their creativity and making their mark on the city.

Hip hop music became a way for people to share their experiences, hopes, and dreams. It became a powerful tool for self-expression and a means to address social and political issues. Many hip hop songs talked about the realities of life in the inner cities, inequality, and the desire for change.

Over time, hip hop spread beyond the Bronx and gained recognition across the United States and the world. It evolved and incorporated various styles, such as rap, R&B, and funk.

Music & Entertainment

Who lives in a pineapple under the sea?

The story of the popular TV show Spongebob Squarepants started with a talented American marine biologist and animator named Stephen Hillenburg, who had a deep love for the ocean and a passion for creating unique and entertaining stories.

One sunny day, as Stephen strolled along the beach, he noticed a sea **sponge** happily **bob**bing along with the waves. Inspired by its cheerful nature and imaginative spirit, an idea sparked in Stephen's mind. He envisioned a world beneath the sea where fascinating creatures lived, and a sponge named SpongeBob would be the star of the show.

With his sketchbook in hand, Stephen began to draw the characters that would inhabit this underwater universe. He created SpongeBob SquarePants, a square-shaped sponge with a contagious smile and an optimistic outlook on life. Alongside SpongeBob, he envisioned his best friend Patrick Star, the lovable but sometimes silly starfish, and Squidward Tentacles, the grumpy but talented clarinet-playing octopus.

Excited about his unique creation, Stephen pitched the idea to television executives,

Music & Entertainment

who were captivated by the colorful characters and imaginative world he had brought to life. They believed that SpongeBob SquarePants had the potential to become something truly special.

On May 1, 1999, SpongeBob SquarePants made its grand debut on television, through Nickelodeon. Children and families everywhere were introduced to the hilarious antics and underwater adventures of SpongeBob and his friends. The show's clever humor, catchy songs, and vibrant animation quickly won the hearts of viewers of all ages.

As the series continued, SpongeBob SquarePants became a cultural phenomenon. Its positive messages of friendship, imagination, and perseverance resonated with audiences around the world. The show's infectious energy and zany characters brought laughter and joy into the lives of millions.

Over the years, SpongeBob SquarePants became more than just a TV show. It inspired movies, video games, and even a Broadway musical. Its lovable characters, like SpongeBob, Patrick, and Squidward, became household names and brought smiles to the faces of fans everywhere.

Music & Entertainment

Mickey Mouse

Once upon a time, in the magical world of animation, a small mouse named Mickey embarked on an extraordinary journey that would change the world of entertainment forever.

It all began in the 1920s when a talented and imaginative artist named Walt Disney had a dream to create a character that would capture the hearts of people around the globe. Inspired by his own experiences and a love for animals, Walt set out to bring this character to life.

One fateful day, as Walt sat at his drawing table, he sketched a mischievous little mouse with round ears, big eyes, and an infectious smile. He knew this mouse had something special, a charm and playfulness that would resonate with audiences of all ages.

Walt named this little mouse Mickey and brought him to the silver screen in a groundbreaking animated short film called "Steamboat Willie." Released on November 18, 1928, this was the first Mickey Mouse cartoon ever created.

Audiences were enthralled as they watched Mickey take on the role of a mischievous deckhand on a steamboat, bringing laughter

Music & Entertainment

and joy to the screen through his lively antics and unforgettable personality. But what truly made "Steamboat Willie" unique was that it was one of the first cartoons to synchronize sound and animation, creating a whole new experience for viewers.

From that moment on, Mickey Mouse became an instant sensation. People fell in love with his charming personality, his adventurous spirit, and his ability to bring laughter and happiness wherever he went. Mickey soon became the iconic symbol of Walt Disney's imagination and the beloved face of a company that would grow to create magical experiences around the world.

With each new adventure, Mickey Mouse captured the hearts of millions, spreading joy through his cartoons, comic books, merchandise, and theme park appearances. His friends, such as Minnie Mouse, Donald Duck, and Goofy, joined him on countless escapades, entertaining audiences and inspiring imaginations.

As the years passed, Mickey Mouse continued to evolve and adapt to new technologies and storytelling techniques. He starred in full-length feature films, appeared on television, and became a global ambassador for happiness and dreams.

Animals & Nature

The Bald Eagle

The bald eagle is a bird that holds great significance for the USA, as it is known as it's national bird and symbol. You might have seen it on the country's flag, coins, and even in many patriotic symbols.

The bald eagle is a large bird with a white head and a brown body. It is known for its majestic appearance and impressive wingspan. It is a powerful and graceful creature that represents strength, freedom, and courage. For a long time, the bald eagle has been a symbol of the United States because it resembles the values and spirit of the country. It is seen as a symbol of freedom, just like the USA itself. The bald eagle is known for its ability to fly high in the sky, representing the freedom to explore, dream, and achieve great things.

The bald eagle is also known for its keen eyesight. It can spot its prey from high above and swoop down to catch it with precision. This sharp vision represents the ability to see things clearly and make wise decisions, which are important qualities for a country's leaders and its people.

Animals & Nature

Mammoth Cave

Deep beneath the rolling hills of Kentucky, there lies a hidden world full of wonder and mystery. It is called Mammoth Cave, and it is an underground marvel that has captivated explorers and adventurers for centuries.
Mammoth Cave is an enormous underground maze of tunnels, chambers, and passageways. It stretches for over 400 miles, making it the longest known cave system in the world! Can you imagine how big that is?
Inside Mammoth Cave, there are countless treasures waiting to be discovered. Stalactites hang from the cave ceilings like icicles, while stalagmites rise from the cave floor, shaped like ancient statues. There are also incredible rock formations like the famous Frozen Niagara, which resembles a frozen waterfall.
As you venture deeper into the cave, you might feel a sense of awe and excitement. The air becomes cool and damp, and you can hear the sounds of dripping water echoing through the tunnels. It's like stepping into a different world altogether.
But Mammoth Cave is not just a place of rock and darkness. It is also home to creepy creatures that have adapted to live in this unique underground habitat. Bats,

Animals & Nature

salamanders, and cave crickets that look like large spiders are just a few of the animals that call Mammoth Cave their home. Throughout history, Mammoth Cave has held a special place in the hearts of people. Native American tribes explored its depths long before European settlers arrived. Today, Mammoth Cave is a national park, protected and preserved for everyone to enjoy. Visitors can take guided tours, led by park rangers, who share stories about the cave's history and geology. They can walk along well-lit paths, admire the stunning formations, and even take a boat ride on the underground rivers.

Alligator!

In the swampy wetlands of the southeastern United States, a magnificent creature lurks beneath the water's surface. It is the American alligator, the largest living reptile in the country and a true marvel of nature.

The American alligator is a formidable creature, known for its massive size and powerful presence. These ancient reptiles can grow up to 15 feet long, with some individuals reaching even greater lengths. Imagine a creature as long as a small car!

Animals & Nature

With their strong, muscular bodies covered in armored scales, American alligators are perfectly adapted for life in the water. Their sharp teeth, often visible when their mouths open wide, are designed for capturing and devouring their prey. While they mainly feed on fish, turtles, birds, and small mammals, they are capable of taking down larger animals when the opportunity arises. One of the most fascinating aspects of the American alligator's life is its habitat. They are found in the southeastern states of the USA, particularly in Florida and Louisiana, where the warm and marshy environment provides an ideal home. These reptiles thrive in freshwater lakes, swamps, rivers, and even brackish estuaries.

The alligator's powerful tail acts as a propeller, allowing it to move swiftly through the water. It often remains submerged, with only its eyes and nostrils visible above the surface, making it an expert at stealthy ambushes. When it's time to cool off or sunbathe, alligators can be seen basking on the banks, their eyes scanning the surroundings for any signs of danger.

Though powerful and sometimes fearsome, the American alligator plays a crucial role in its ecosystem. As apex predators, they help

Animals & Nature

regulate the populations of other species and maintain a healthy balance in their habitats. Their presence ensures the diversity and stability of the wetland ecosystems they call home.

People have long been captivated by the allure of these magnificent creatures. Alligator sightings and encounters in their natural habitats can be an exciting and educational experience, as long as they are observed from a safe distance. It's important to remember that these creatures are wild and should be respected for their power and natural instincts.

Yellowstone

Yellowstone National Park was the first national park established in the United States. It was created in 1872 to protect its unique features and the amazing wildlife that called it home. The park covers a vast area of over 2 million acres, with forests, mountains, rivers, and even a supervolcano! One of the most famous attractions in Yellowstone is the world-renowned Old Faithful geyser. It shoots hot water and steam high up into the sky at regular intervals, thrilling visitors with its spectacular displays. People from all over

Animals & Nature

the world gather around to watch this natural wonder in action.

But that's not all! Yellowstone is also home to many other geysers, hot springs, and colorful pools. You can see the Grand Prismatic Spring, which is the largest hot spring in the United States and has blues, oranges, and greens, making it look like a watercolor painting.

As you explore the park, you might come across herds of bison, which are some of the largest land animals in North America. These majestic creatures roam freely through the grasslands, chewing on grass and sometimes causing a little traffic jam as they cross the roads. It's an amazing sight to see! You might also spot elk grazing by the rivers, playful otters splashing in the water, or even catch a glimpse of a grizzly bear or a wolf. Just don't forget not to go too close to them!

If you love waterfalls, Yellowstone won't disappoint! You can visit the mesmerizing Lower Falls, which cascades down into the canyon, creating a breathtaking sight. The rushing water and the surrounding cliffs will make you feel like you're in a magical world.

Animals & Nature

As you venture deeper into the park, you'll be surrounded by towering mountains and dense forests. You can hike along the trails, breathing in the fresh mountain air and enjoying the peacefulness of nature. You might come across beautiful wildflowers, hidden meadows, or even a hidden gem like a secret waterfall.

Yellowstone is not just a park, it's a playground for adventurers and nature lovers. It's a place where you can connect with the wonders of the natural world and be in awe of its beauty. So, grab your binoculars, pack your backpack, and get ready for an unforgettable journey in Yellowstone National Park. You never know what surprises await you around the next bend!

Record breaking Wood

The US is home to some of the oldest and tallest trees in the world. The petrified forest in the USA is a park where wood from over 200 million years ago remains to this day! The wood is so old, that it has actually turned to stone, and it is a very unusual sight to see.

In California, some of the tallest trees exist in the redwood forests. Some trees, particularly to famous giant sequoia trees

Animals & Nature

are over 300 feet (100 meters) tall and have been alive for thousands of years!

Florida Coral Reef

You have probably heard about the Great Barrier Reef in Australia, but did you know that Florida also has its very own coral reef? Deep beneath the sparkling turquoise waters of Florida, a hidden world of wonder awaits. These coral reefs, where a vibrant underwater paradise thrives with life and color, are a haven for a diverse array of marine creatures, creating an underwater kingdom like no other.

As you descend beneath the surface, you are greeted by an explosion of colors. The coral reefs are alive with a kaleidoscope of colors, ranging from brilliant blues and vibrant yellows to stunning pinks and mesmerizing purples. These colors come from the corals themselves, which build complex structures that provide shelter and food for a vast array of marine life.

Alongside the colors of the coral itself are a wide selection of colorful fish, the angel fish and even the famous clownfish from Finding Nemo!

Animals & Nature

A Grand Canyon

The USA is home to one of the most famous canyons, the grand canyon. Situated in the Mojave desert, it stretches over 277 miles, and offers amazing views. The Grand Canyon was formed millions of years ago when rivers flowed across the land, slowly carving their way through layers of rock over countless centuries. The forces of nature worked tirelessly, shaping and sculpting the earth, until a magnificent canyon emerged.
The layers of rock that make up the Grand Canyon tell a fascinating tale of the Earth's history. As you venture deeper into the canyon, you travel back in time, passing through millions of years of geological history. Each layer holds clues about the ancient seas, deserts, and forests that once covered this land.

Thats Hot!

Not far from the grand canyon, in a place called death valley, the hottest temperature on Earth was recorded in 1913 at 134 °F (56.7 °C)!

Food & Drink

McDonalds, anyone?

McDonald's is a famous fast food restaurant that you may have heard of or even visited with your family. It all started a long time ago in 1940, when two brothers named Richard and Maurice McDonald opened a small restaurant in California, United States.
At first, their restaurant was called "McDonald's Bar-B-Q," and they served delicious barbecued food. But over time, they realized that people really loved their hamburgers, so they decided to change their focus and make hamburgers their main menu item.
The brothers wanted to make their restaurant faster and more efficient, so they came up with a clever system. They created a special way of making hamburgers called the "Speedee Service System." This system made it possible to serve food quickly and with high quality, giving birth to fast food in America, and across the world.
One day, a man named Ray Kroc visited the McDonald brothers' restaurant. He was so impressed with their system that he had an idea. He thought, "Why not open more McDonald's restaurants all over the country?"
Ray Kroc worked closely with the McDonald

Food & Drink

brothers and together they built the first franchised McDonald's restaurant in Illinois. Franchised means that other people could open their own McDonald's restaurants using the same system and recipes.

As more and more McDonald's restaurants opened, they became very popular. People loved the tasty hamburgers, the fast service, and the fun Happy Meals that came with toys. McDonald's grew and grew, and today it is one of the biggest and most well-known fast food chains in the world.

Who invented the hamburger?

Why is the burger called a hamburger if it's not made out of ham? The answer is because the hamburger is named after Hamburg, a German city.

At that time, Hamburg was a busy seaport, filled with sailors and travelers from around the world. The sailors would often bring back minced beef from their journeys, which was considered a delicacy. The meat was seasoned and shaped into patties, then cooked to perfection.

As time went on, the concept of the "Hamburg-style steak" made its way to the United States, carried by German immigrants who sought new opportunities and a better

Food & Drink

Popular American Food

Heres some of the food Americans enjoy:

- American pancakes are fluffy and often served with maple syrup and butter. They are a popular breakfast choice for many families
- The hot dog is a classic American food. It is a sausage served in a long bun and is often topped with ketchup, mustard, onions, and other condiments.
- The USA is famous for its delicious barbecue. Different regions have their own styles, such as Texas-style brisket, Carolina-style pulled pork, and Kansas City-style ribs.
- American chocolate chip cookies are loved around the world. They are soft, chewy cookies with chunks of chocolate in every bite.
- Root beer is a popular non-alcoholic drink in the USA. It has a distinct, sweet, and slightly spicy flavor and is often enjoyed with ice cream in a float.
- Peanut butter and jelly (jam) sandwiches are a staple in many American households. They are made by spreading peanut butter and jelly (jam) between two slices of bread! If you have not tried this, you have to.

Food & Drink

- The USA is known for its love of pizza. It is a favorite food for many Americans, with various toppings like cheese, pepperoni, vegetables, and more.
- Americans enjoy a variety of snacks, including potato chips, popcorn, pretzels, and corn dogs. These snacks are often enjoyed during movie nights or as quick bites on-the-go.

An Energizing Drink

Once upon a time, in the town of Atlanta, Georgia, there lived a man named John Pemberton. He was a pharmacist and had a knack for inventing new medicines and concoctions. One day, he came up with a special recipe that would become the origins of a famous drink we now know as Coca-Cola. It was the year 1886, and John Pemberton was experimenting in his laboratory. He mixed together various ingredients like coca leaves, cola nuts, and other secret flavors to create a unique, refreshing and energizing drink.

One hot summer day, Pemberton decided to test his new creation. He poured the dark, fizzy liquid into a glass and took a sip. To his delight, it tasted delicious! It was sweet, with a hint of caramel and a fizzy

Food & Drink

sensation that tickled the tongue. Pemberton realized he had created something special, a drink that tasted refreshing and also had a spark inside. He decided to share his invention with others, and that's how Coca-Cola was born.

At first, Coca-Cola was sold as a syrup that people could mix with water at home. It became popular in Atlanta, and soon word spread about this magical drink. People loved its unique taste and the way it made them feel refreshed and energized.

At the time, little was known about the effects of cocaine, so it was not illegal, and the original recipe actually contained cocaine from the coca leaves.

Over the years, Coca-Cola continued to spread its refreshing taste around the world, but as the recipe was modified to remove the coca leaves. Fortunately, the flavor was still great, and quickly became a favorite drink for people of all ages, bringing smiles and happiness wherever it was enjoyed.

Food Fun

When it comes to food, the United States is known for its bold and sometimes wacky

Food & Drink

culinary creations. From state fairs to quirky restaurants, the USA has gained a reputation for its unusual and unique food inventions that push the boundaries of creativity.

One such invention that has gained popularity at state fairs and carnivals is the deep-fried Oreo. This dessert takes the classic chocolate cookie and dips it into a sweet batter before deep-frying it to golden perfection. The result is a warm, crispy exterior that gives way to a gooey, melted, chocolaty center.

But the wackiness doesn't stop there. A beverage gaining popularity is the bacon-flavored soda. This intriguing concoction combines the smoky, savory taste of bacon with the fizzy sweetness of soda. It's an unusual flavor combination that you definitely have to try.

Possibly the most unusual creation that has taken state fairs by storm is deep-fried butter. Yes, you read that right. Imagine a stick of butter, dipped in a batter and then deep fried until golden. What results is a crispy shell with a completely melted center. Deep fried butter can be enjoyed with a drizzle of syrup on top or powedered sugar.

Culture

The American Dream

The American Dream is a very special idea that many people believe in. It's the belief that in America, anyone can have a chance to make their dreams come true and have a better life. It's like a big, exciting adventure!

Imagine you have a dream, something that you really want to achieve or become in your life. Maybe you want to be a doctor, a teacher, an artist, or even an astronaut. The American Dream says that if you work hard, set goals, and never give up, you have the opportunity to make your dream a reality.

In America, people believe that everyone should be treated fairly and have equal opportunities to succeed. It doesn't matter where you come from, what your family is like, or what you look like. The American Dream is all about believing in yourself and working hard to reach your goals.

Many people come to America from different countries because they believe in the American Dream. They hope to create a better life for themselves and their families. They want to have the chance to get a good education, find a job they love, and have a happy and fulfilling life.

Culture

The American Dream is not just about being successful or making a lot of money. It's also about having the freedom to express yourself, follow your passions, and contribute to your community. It's about being kind, helping others, and making the world a better place.

But remember, the American Dream doesn't mean everything will be easy. It means that you might face challenges along the way. Sometimes, you may fail or face obstacles, but that's okay. The important thing is to keep trying, keep learning, and never give up on your dreams.

So, whether you were born in America or come from a different place, you can believe in the American Dream. It's a wonderful idea that tells us that with hard work, determination, and a positive attitude, you can achieve great things and make your dreams come true.

Always remember, you are the captain of your own ship, and the American Dream is there to inspire you to set sail on a journey full of possibilities. Dream big, work hard, and believe in yourself. The American Dream is waiting for you!

Culture

American English

Throughout the world, it is often American English that we hear spoken on TV or in movies or in video games, but did you there are quite some differences between American English and British English? Here are just a few:

- Sidewalk vs. Pavement: When walking along the side of the road, Americans call it a "sidewalk," while the British refer to it as "pavement."
- Cookie vs. Biscuit: Americans use the word "cookie" for a sweet baked treat, while the British use the word "biscuit." However, it's important to note that American biscuits are similar to British scones.
- Gasoline vs. Petrol: In the United States, the fuel used for cars is called "gasoline," while in Britain it is called "petrol."
- Soccer vs. Football: In the United States, the sport where players kick a round ball into a net is called "soccer." In Britain, it is known as "football." However, American football and British football (soccer) are different sports.
- Trash vs. Rubbish: Americans use the word "trash" to refer to waste or garbage, while the British use the word "rubbish."

Culture

- Vacation vs. Holiday: Americans refer to a period of time when they take a break from school or work as a "vacation." In Britain, they use the word "holiday" to describe the same thing.
- Candy vs. Sweets: Americans use the word "candy" to describe sugary treats, while the British use the word "sweets."
- Fries vs. Chips: In the USA, thin, crispy slices of potatoes are called "French fries." In Britain, they are known as "chips." British "chips" are closer to what Americans call "thick-cut fries."
- Diaper vs. Nappy: In the United States, a baby's undergarment is called a "diaper," whereas in Britain it is referred to as a "nappy."
- Sneakers vs. Trainers: Americans use the word "sneakers" to describe athletic shoes, while the British use the term "trainers."
- Cell phone vs. Mobile phone: In the USA, people commonly refer to a portable telephone as a "cell phone," whereas in Britain it is called a "mobile phone."
- Faucet vs. Tap: Americans refer to a device for controlling the flow of water as a "faucet," while the British call it a "tap."

Culture

- Jelly vs. Jam: In America, "jelly" refers to a clear, fruit-based spread without any fruit pieces - it is often used in peanut butter and jelly sandwiches. The British call this jam. What the British call "jelly" as in the wobbly dessert is known in the USA as "jello".
- Trunk vs. Boot: In America, the "trunk" of a car refers to the storage compartment at the back of the vehicle for storing luggage and other items. The British call this the "boot".
- Fall vs Autumn: The season before winter is normally called "fall" in the USA, but is called "autumn" in the UK.
- Yard vs. Garden: In the USA, a "yard" typically refers to the outdoor area surrounding a house. In the UK, it is called a "garden".

Culture

Why Guns?

You may have seen that the USA of all countries have a lot of guns, but why is that? The reasoning goes back to when the USA was born and the constitution, that contains laws, has a law that is known as the Second Amendment. It says: "A well-regulated Militia, being necessary to the security of a free State, the right of the people to keep and bear Arms, shall not be infringed." In other words, people are allowed to carry guns to protect their country.

It may seem weird now, but it made sense when the USA was just formed and won in a difficult war against Britain.

The Founding Fathers, who were the leaders of the young nation, wanted to make sure that the people had certain rights and protections.

One of these rights was to own and carry weapons, such as guns. The Founding Fathers believed that this right was important for the people to protect themselves and their families, and also to defend the country if necessary.

During that time, the United States had just fought a war for independence against Britain, and they wanted to ensure that the

Culture

government would not become too powerful and take away the people's freedoms. They believed that the ability for citizens to have arms would help prevent that from happening.

The idea behind the Second Amendment was to allow the people to form militias, which are groups of citizens who are trained in using weapons and can come together to protect their communities. The Founding Fathers believed that having a well-regulated militia would help ensure the security of the new country.

In modern times, different opinions and discussions continue about how to balance the rights of individuals with the need for a safe environment.

Also Check Out...

INTERESTING FACTS & STORIES THROUGHOUT HISTORY
For Curious Kids!

- WHAT IS THE FORBIDDEN CITY?
- WHATS THE STORY OF LIEF ERIKSON?
- WHO WERE THE SPARTA?
- WHY DID WE BUILD PYRAMIDS?

FIVE MILE PUBLICATIONS

www.ingramcontent.com/pod-product-compliance
Lightning Source LLC
Chambersburg PA
CBHW030039100526
44590CB00011B/268